BLACK MAN IN EUROPE

BY NATHAN JONES

SAJETANIRA PUBLISHING GROUP

P.O. Box 211-0211
Oakland, CA 94604
www.sajetanirapublishing.com

Printed in the USA

Library of Congress Cataloging-in-Publication Data
Jones, Nathan
Black Man In Europe/Nathan Jones

Edited by Corey Edward Olds and Charlotte Y. Williams
Book design by Design Action Collective
ISBN: 978-0-9800747-0-3 (pbk: alk. paper)

Acknowledgment:

This project is dedicated to all those individuals
who believed in my ability and talent.

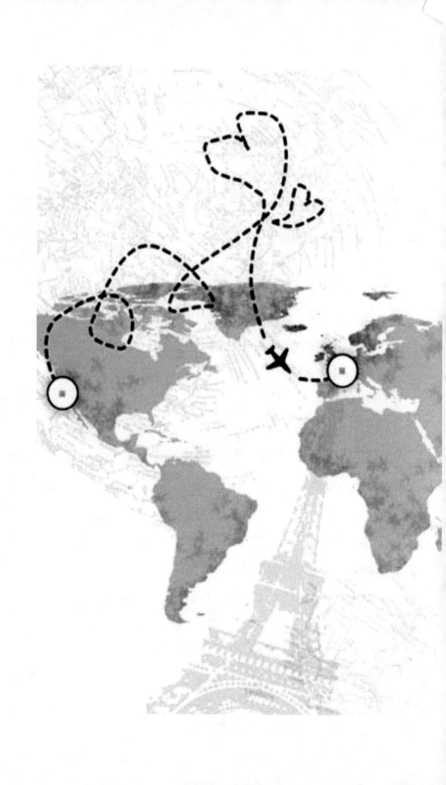

CONTENTS

DOWN AT NIGHT

The Bible was fulfilling itself as I silently trembled, watching out of the window overlooking Rue de Bergère. God was admonishing his people with calamitous and deceptive changes of season. Lightning flashed out of the east, heaven and earth seemed to pass away. Outside there were two in the street, and one was taken, and the other left. Inside, at the well of drinks, one was spared, the other, not.

Charcoal was the sky, something out of Poe. The floodgates of heaven beat the earth like a Senegalese, his djimbé. Still, my mind wandered back to the softness of her voice; to the sweetness of her perfume (divinity must smell like this).

I lie in her bosom, warm and nurtured as a child. She fills my ear with spiritual salve, soothing as a mother's love. Sheltered from inclemency, I daydreamed about the day I would finally arrive in Europe. And here I am.

Following Richard Wright, Chester Himes, James Baldwin, Josephine Baker, Sidney Bechet, and Lois Mailou Jones, I am here to finally receive acknowledgement for my talents, person, character, and humanity. I am here, in Paris, to create novellas, vignettes, stories, prose, and romantic poetry. I am here to lounge in cafés, to comb the Latin Quarter, to stare out at the River Seine. I am here to sip old vines. I am here to sport a black beret tilted roguishly, a cashmere sweater over my shoulders, grey flannel on my legs, suede loafers couching my feet.

This dream of Paris is not new, neither the one about Bordeaux or the Côte d'Azur.

Then, years ago, the fresh smell of jasmine and clover filled Mama Enola's kitchen, as I dreamed. The kitchen inside the 1930s

Victorian that Grandpa remodeled over the course of two summers and one fall, relying on carpentry skills that he never had to learn.

Mama Enola's homemade peach cobbler and her famous tea cakes, that she would make for all her grandchildren, and would sell on occasion, when family members needed financial help, were cooling off in the window pane. I was lost in thought.

In another time, in another place, Yani was listening intently, reacting with her hands, screwing her eyes, every now and then running her fingers through my locks.

"Why this talk of Europe so much? And what is your fascination with this European lifestyle?" she stormed.

"Baby, it's been calling me since I was eighteen, and I can't let that voice go, not until I know what it is. It's part of my destiny."

"Well, are you going to take me, or do you expect me to wait for you?" Yani protested.

"I hope you wait because it's something I have to do by myself," I tried to explain. She turned and left the room. I continued to sit and reminisce about my first trip to Europe. I feel my feet touching the ground at Gare du Nord. I hear the euphony of French. I see Renaults, Citroêns, and wide, tree-lined boulevards.

Who would ever have thought that a boy from East Oakland, by way of Assumption Parish, would come face to face with his dream? The first time my feet touched French soil, I felt higher than Kaya and the Holy Ghost combined. That high never completely left, it lingers in my lungs and loins, fortifies my blood. Being there was like a boy's first kiss, a virgin's first love, and the more I experienced, the more I wanted more.

As I was relishing all of this, Yani came back into the room. She moved closer to me than before. She began to ask me a series of why's and what's.

"What will you find in Europe that you don't already have here?" she lamented.

"Freedom, peace of mind, respect as a human being, and acknowledgement of my craft."

Yani did not seem to understand that once a Black intellectual crosses the ocean blue, he or she quits Tally's Corner, slays Jim Crow, and climbs life to find no ceilings – at least there is the hope of it. He or she slowly realizes that art is its own reward, a ladder to ethereal modes, to places that efficient, hardworking, monotonous souls rarely see, let alone taste.

There is more to life than survival than sterling credentials. I always hear the voice of ancestors saying, "Do better than we did. Create a legacy for yourself and your children". I told Yani that I wanted my legacy to begin with art. At these words, Yani opened up, a little.

We talked for hours that night. I told her of my Spanish flat in Barcelona. It was located on the fifth floor of an apartment nearly one hundred and twenty years old, in the heart of Barcelona, near C/D en Blanco 54, 2-2, a block from the metro for Plaza de Sants (running off the red and blue lines).

For two weeks I had no hot water. I showered with cold water in a half-sized tub. At certain hours of the day, the city smelled like dead fish and garbage. Every night, I slept nude because of the heat, not to mention the humidity. While the city partied all night, I studied in quiet isolation like a monk in my garret (a regular Benedictine was I).

It was surreal to me. I did not know the language. I did not know the cultural codes. Nor did I know how impersonal Spanish were. None of those things mattered though. For, as Chester Himes said, "No matter what I did or how I lived, I had considered myself a writer . . . It was my salvation. The world can deny me all other employment, and stone me as an ex-convict . . . as a disagreeable, unpleasant person. But as long as I write, whether it's published or not, I'm a writer." And that's exactly how I feel.

Deep Soulful Eyes

You are *lifetimes manifested*
6000 years of mother wit
Eyes are *Heaven's* constellations, illuminating
Deep soulful eyes piercing my essence and existence
You are *Nandi's, Sheba's*, and *Nzinga's lamentations*
Reigning and raining on *Earth's* embryonic creations.
A micro-cosmic expression of you, I am.
Reflecting the spiritual-physical, metaphysical
manifestation
Image...image...images...of...God/Dess, Goddess...
...Imagine me...
A reflection of your effervescence,   reminiscent,
consistent
Blessings *reincarnated* over time, your seed, human
and *divine*
Arcs of love filling my soul with celestial
treasures,
The MA'AT I represent, a wingspan on 42
precepts/principles inscribed
Deep soulful eyes welcome me, as I can come inside
Your sanctuary and lie in your lap wisdom and
knowledge.
Deep soulful eyes speak to me in your *language* of
divinity.
Invite me in, tune me in, and never let me go,
Until our *Creator* returns home for *His* second
coming.
Deep soulful eyes, be my *high* and *pride*.
Eyes soulful and vast, bless me! bless me! cover
me!

Release me back to myself as Sankofa returns me
Back to the sanctity and solidarity of my
mother's womb.
Soulful eyes, you are infinite lifetimes manifested!

Starry Nights

Wo'set pillars are aligned perfectly with the
Constellations
Perfection is knowing our "universe' is sacred like
biblical scripture
Memories are the pearls, which give way to
wisdom and knowledge
Freudian dreams aren't models for timeless
discussion
We are the time capsules-the love designs we create
We learn from Shakespearean tales of
tragedy/comedy
Othello's deceptions, suspending our disbelief
Time is paradise, man's sanctuary on Earth
Each second a year
Each minute a decade
Each hour a century
Experiences we can and cannot fathom
We find each other like spirits passing through
night
We seek and search for ourselves at the bottom
of the well
Reflections of distorted watered mirror images
Tapestries designing our Asili, cultivating our
loneliness

While love becomes a sacrificial possibility, that jars our souls
Unfamiliar yet once visited in remote times pass
We pass on fulfillment, affairs of what might become
Like is ephemeral like sand castles
A touch like an anachronism
We fit like an angel apexing a Christmas tree
We revel in aphorisms, brief statements of truth
You become my aphelion, a planetary orbit farthest away from me
Your sun, I remember the night

ENGLAND:
BILL SIKES

It is 1998, a Tuesday, mid-evening. My flight on Virgin Atlantic has just landed at Heathrow International Airport. I am extremely excited, tired, and nervous. However, there is one bit of good tiding: everything is in English, therefore I do not have to switch my tongue back and forth from French.

London appears to be a very beautiful city, so far. But like any metropolis, the illusion is always what you see first: the elegant shops, the monuments of marble, the financial district, the blue ribbon restaurants, and the good side of life. One can fall in love with these first impressions.

Of course, London has an underbelly: ethnically segregated areas, ghettos, the tenderloin, and squalid industrial wastelands (unfit for even rats). Though, I am looking forward to seeing Brixton, Eastham, Tottenham, and those parts of the city where people reside who look like me.

Until now, England and the English were stuff mediated through Shakespeare, Dickens, and Sherlock Holmes. England was also music: the Beatles, the Rolling Stones, and the pop rock groups of the eighties. Of course, England was the Parliament, Queen Elizabeth, Prince Charles, and Lady Diana. However, I wanted to know less about the royalty and the trappings of English high culture, and more about the commoners, especially those of African descent.

This backpacking trip marks my first to Europe and England is the first stop. Like any newcomer, I will quickly learn the ins-and-outs of the city. I will have to find the International House on Great

Portland Street where I will be lodging for a few days. To get there, I will take the Underground.

I will need to find the best place to exchange money. I will need to learn how to make a phone call and where to dine cheaply. Eventually, I will head to my cousin's flat in Tottenham, and stay a few days before crossing the Channel into France.

London reminds me of back home, San Francisco: it is rainy and misty like there. I feel foolish having just left The City where the rain had drowned months, to end up on another continent where the gray drowns more months.

I retrieved my personal items from the overhead compartment, checked for all my vitals (passport, identification, money, travel guides, etc). Before heading to the front, I collected my faculties, took a long sigh and a stretch. Very slowly, more than two hundred of us trod the aisle, after ten and one-half hours across the Atlantic.

As I am about to alight, the flight attendants and the pilots promptly bid adieu.

"We hope you have enjoyed your flight. Thanks for flying Virgin Airlines," they chime in mechanical unison.

"And thank you for a safe and wonderful trip," I reply.

Having left the plane, headed toward baggage claim, it dawned upon me that those were the sexiest flight attendants I had ever seen. They were right out of a movie. I smiled a Chester Himes smile, glad to have had a Virgin flight. Better-than-average food, superb service, good movies, and beautiful women conspired to seduce me.

Walking through Heathrow, I was astounded by its size. Most incredible were the three different terminals leading to three different rail platforms. After the long trek from the airplane to baggage claim to retrieve my oversized pack, I was directed to stand in the visitor's line at the customs gate. During the wait, I noticed that I had been the only person of color on the flight. Though I should not have been surprised, I still could not believe it: I, the only bird of my stripe flying the friendly skies.

I reached the customs counter sooner than expected. I dug into my blue Howard University windbreaker and pulled out my passport. I handed it to the customs agent. He looked it over and began to fire away.

"How are you Mr. Jones?"

"Fine, thank you."

"Are you traveling alone?"

"Yes."

"How long do you plan to be in England?

"I shall be here for a week."
"And shall you be visiting anyone here?"

"I shall visit a relative."

"Enjoy your trip!"

"Thank you, I shall indeed."

The customs agent stamped my passport before handing it back, and I walked off in search of the Underground. I felt like an immigrant who had just docked on Ellis Island in New York. About the Underground I knew nothing, not even how to get there. And, even once I found it, I still had no idea of which train to catch to the International Student House located near the Great Portland Street exit.

Fortunately, there are maps, and this one was in English. I kept looking at the signs above me, making sure as I walked through the airport, that I was headed toward the Underground. And I was, for I eventually reached it.

According to the map, I was to take the Piccadilly line, then transfer to the Circle (Yellow Line), and travel east to Great Portland. Sitting at the Piccadilly line, the train arrived in approximately ten minutes. I boarded en route to the International Student House.

I heard an automated voice saying, "Mind the gap." I started to laugh. I knew what the warning referred to, but it was so strange to hear it phrased in John Bull's English. As I sat down, I realized that the ISH was approximately twenty-four stops away, quite a distance.

I made it to the Circle (Yellow Line), and waited for the next train to come. After a long thirty-five-minute ride, I got off the train, ascended three flights of stairs, and to my surprise, I was exactly one block away from the International Student House.

Through the misty showers, I took my time to the ISH. I was somewhat refreshed. The Underground ride had been a dirty one. I peered all around, taking in everything that I could. The sights were amazing. Students flocked everywhere, and on every corner, there was a bank. The English were definitely about their money.

Into the ISH, I approached the receptionist counter. Behind it stood a young Brit. She sported a spiked, blonde butch, heavy-eyeliner, a tube of lipstick, and a leather bodice crisscrossed with chains. Actually, she was a throwback to the eighties punk rock era. She stared at me and I stared back. Before I could say anything, she spoke very quickly with a thick accent that clogged my ears.

"Can I help you?" she asked with a slight attitude. But I did not care.

"Yes, you may. I have reservations for the next three days. I paid in advance."

"Okay, let me check the reservation list. "Uhhh . . ." she searched for my information.

"What is your name and do you have your ID and/or your international student ID?" she inquired.

"Yes, I have everything you need. Here's my passport, my student ID, and my reservation receipt."

"Okay, sir. I see that all has checked out. Let me get you a key to your room."

"Thank you."

"Sir, I need to inform you that you will be sharing a room with three other people. Is that okay with you?"

"Have I a choice?"

"No. Unfortunately, all rooms are shared. But do enjoy your stay, and if you need anything, consult your ISH guide. It will tell you everything you require: office hours for the front desk, when breakfast is served, and the amenities offered by ISH."

"Thank you very much. I will look into it."

Leaving the front area of the ISH, I realized that my room would not be easy to find. The hallways were a maze, the envy of Dadaelus' labyrinth that concealed the Minotaur. A string of corridors, left, right, left, right, straight, around the corner, right, left, right, go back to the left, right?

After walking what seemed to be an eternity, I found my room. I went to the door, inserted the key, and entered. I could not believe my eyes. It was a military bunker. There were two sets of bunk beds, two metal closets, and four concrete walls.

As I got situated, trying to make myself as comfortable as possible, I decided to take the top bunk, to the right side of the room, closest to the door. Like a wave of ocean crashing upon my back, a strong feeling of nervousness and insecurity suddenly came over me. I abhorred the energy in the room. I considered my roommates weirdoes.

To lighten the situation, I began to introduce myself. I had to establish my territory. I wanted to create the illusion that I was a veteran traveler, and that I harbored no fear or discontent at being in a room full of strangers. Summoning my American confidence, I started in.

"What's up guys, I'm Anthony, from the USA."

"Hello Anthony, I'm Mark, from Canada."

"Allo, Anthony, I'm John, from Australia." John's accent proved thicker than that of the receptionist. John, I'd admit, had me a bit spooked from his appearance alone. His energy reeked of a potential serial killer. Although he tried subtly to intimidate me with his insane skinhead stir, I could not show any signs of fear. So, I put on my Oakland Black Panther face to parry any sense that he was bigger or badder than me.

"Hello Anthony, I'm Simon, from New Zealand."

"Good to meet you fellows. It's a pleasure," I said firmly.

Finally, I felt more comfortable. I dropped my backpack to the floor, and began to place my things in one of the portable closets. I finished quickly, and ventured back to the main area of the ISH. I carried my pack with me, leaving it in a safety holding room, where it seemed like every pack in London lounged. Returning to the front desk, I noticed a picture of Jomo Kenyatta, the former African leader of Kenya, hanging behind the counter. Funny, I had not noticed it earlier. Had Kenyatta spent some time at the ISH? If so, then I felt in good company, and for the first time since landing at Heathrow.

Time was really moving fast. Before I knew it, one o'clock struck, and people were still rambling about. I decided to go to the front desk to buy a BC card. This card would give me pay-phone access to call stateside. I had to tell my mother that I had safely made the trip to London.

Mothers tend to be overly concerned about their children, and my mother is certainly no exception. My mother made me promise to call her upon arriving at each of my destinations, and to leave all of the contact information. So, like a good son, I called and left a fully detailed message.

Next, hunger called me, and I ventured out for the first time. Strolling down Great Portland Street, excitement overtook my senses and I felt transformed as if I were a werewolf. The London special mantled me. The north side of the Thames pleased my sense of elegance.

Surrounding me were Bobbies and beefeaters. My mind recalled Masterpiece Theater and "London Bridge is falling down." Red double-decker buses whirled uncontrollably around Piccadilly Circus. I followed them and experienced vertigo.

Strolling in the outpost of advancing day, I wanted to see all of London's landmarks, but 'twas late. Regents Park,. London Zoo, the West End, the British Museum, and Big Ben reluctantly drew me forth, though Super-Ego urged me to return to the ISH and to partake of the stale fare of bar and grill. But I am propelled by ubiquitous footsteps and enticed by carousing cheer.

By the time I reach Leicester Square, I am full – to the point of overload – with Mayfair refinement and tourist entrapments. My Ego or my Id – I do not know which – tells me that food can wait, that now is the time to see the lions.

So I stroll, but before I can take two steps, strangers approach, two of them hem me in. They pat their coat and pants pockets.

"What's up lad? What's up laddie boy, where are you going t-night?" Yeah, lad, what do have for us?" the other prods.

They start tugging on my clothes. I am shocked. On my first night in London, these two pricks are trying to mug me. They are also trying to assault my manhood, for they keep calling me lad. I swing Jack Johnson blows to their heads, and they back out of the way.

"Muthafucka, don't ever put your hands on me," I exclaim, still swinging and moving forward. I cuff the tall one on the ear, and ask him low large does a "lad" grow in London, England."

"Lad" echoed in my head, and I thought back to my grandmother. Once a New Orleans pig stopped my grandmother and grandfather and called my grandfather a "boy." Wittily but angrily, my grandmother asked the pig, "How large does a "boy" grow in your country?" Language and individual words may change over time, but some words retain their original meaning, power, and violence.

"Give us some money lad," the tall once said, feeling his ear for blood, "or we're going to carve you into a bloody pulp."

"If you're bold enough to cut me, then you'd better kill me because if you don't, the peelers will find both of you stinking in the morning."

The tall one was bluffing, but the short, barrel-chested one with a scar on his cheek kept scanning the street, his right hand tensely holding something inside his coat. We stood there for what seemed like hours. I tightened my fists and shuffled to the right, keeping the taller one between Tom Thumb and me. I pulled back and faked with my right, meantime shooting a lightning left to the tall one's chin. Tall buckled back into Tom, nearly knocking him over. Then Tom longed at me – all I saw was a flash of silver in the streetlight.

I backed away, this time keeping Tom between Tall and me. With my right hand, I noticed that my leather had been cut through, cleanly. I heard the footsteps of passersby coming up the street and availed of that opportunity.

"What in the bloody hell are you doing?!?" I yelled. "Get your thieving, Bill Sikes' hands off of me! My words became weapons. But they rushed me anyway, one high, the other low. The knife pressed my side and I did not know what to do. I feared that If I yelled again, the little one would stab me right above my hipbone. The few pedestrians were still about seventy-five yards away.

What to do? I feigned like I was fainting, and as they both struggled to hold me up, the knife flew loose, and before either of them could grab it, I kicked it across the street. The knife, some version of a bowie, sounded plangently, a metal lamentation of unrequited assault.

While my assailants focused on the knife, I brought my right fist to my chest, formed a tight elbow, and caught Tall in the Adam's apple. His knees bent too much and he fell to the ground, choking. Tom started to run for the knife, but I kicked at him, tripping him up, and he skidded on the asphalt.

Immediately I ran over to him and stomped him about the groin, arms, legs, chest, head, spine, back. "Don't you ever put your hands on me, you British bitch!"

Tall had one hand on the ground, trying to get up, but he was severely gasping for air.

The passersby rushed to the scene and looked at my two assailants, then looked at me. Their faces suggested that they knew I was a foreigner from my dress and accent. They also seemed to understand that I had rather emphatically resolved the situation lying before them.

During that brief moment of silence, I felt calm and justified, though my anger, nervousness, and frustration had not completely abated. The two men and three women stood stock-still as if in disbelief.

I turned and headed back to the ISH. When I arrived back to my military bunker, all I could ponder was rest, and allowing my spirit to dissolve my recent encounter with the riff-raff outside. I thought to myself, if this is any indication as to what I am to expect from Europe, then I am in for a beautifully fantastically unexpected journey. Carpe diem!

Great Portland Street

The West End of London, Great Portland Street
Formally known as the City of Westminster
(c.1540),
A borough of London,
North of the River Thames,
Busy and thirsty for non-stop foot traffic,
transient community, non-fluff
A historic trailblazing Duke
Developer and owner the eastern half
Controller of Marylebone strong-holding the 18th
and 19th centuries
BBC Radio,
Yalding House,
Number one Newsbeat,
Not the Guardian, yet influential international
reporting
I wonder sometimes, what this looked like
centuries ago before my arrival
What did the city smell like?
How high were peoples' personal garbage piles?
How long did it take to sanitize the River Thames
for fish to breathe and live naturally, again?
Were there other sources of fresh water to
drink?
Or did they import wine from French vineyards?

Curiosity lurks, as I imagine what the German
composer Felix Mendelssohn Compositions sounded
like.

Were his melodic sounds justified because of his
birth in this Romantic epoch,
Reflecting timeless sensation?
Were smells from the city inspires languid
symphonies, concertos, oratorios, piano, and
chamber music? Or did Fingal's Cave eerie watery
echoes serve as teacher to give natural
atmospheric cathedral sound, to his sound?
Great Portland Street had a silent history to
share, although foreign to me.

Aqua Fresh!

Buckets of rain fall from heaven
Leaving eternal and indelible impressions on
humanity
Adam's lost paradise and Noah's vice,
Waters of heaven and hell continue to devastate
my days
Complementing nature's imperfections, my body
encapsulates
God's pleasure
His beauty
His wrath
Causing conjecture to overwhelm my inner-spirit
Gray clouds of inquiries perpetuate depths of
endless rivers of
ambiguities
Here I stand wet once again,
Swimming in the same cesspool of liquid
uncertainty,
Only to be greeted with endless unrest.
El Nino and grayish dismal overcast, I thought I
left in The Bay Area
Tell me Lord, will this season of rain cease to
alleviate?
Or will it turn over souls like unstable gravesites in
a New Orleans cemetery?

GERMANY: KASSEL

It was a hard morning, trying once again to prepare myself for another trek across Europe. After all, I was leaving one of the most intriguing cities on the Continent. If it had been possible, I would have extended my trip well into the weekend, but my next adventure played my heart like a harp.

The night before, I had promised my friend Teresa, a stunningly beautiful Afro-Asian-Jamaican sister, that I would rendezvous with her in Paris. Teresa was originally from New York, but now she resided in the City of Lights. As fate would have it, my plans got changed. Moreover, my mind was set on other escapades. I wanted to see what the Eastern Europeans lived like, and just how different the cultural experience would be, especially seeing as how I did not speak German.

I would be taking one of the famous, world-class ICE trains. Recently, one of the ICE trains skipped the tracks and collided with a freight train. But it was too late to turn back now. And, if collisions were not enough to vex me, Kassel being the home of the Nazis did. I consoled myself thinking of Hansel, my one contact there.

Packing for such trips is always a Herculean labor: organizing souvenirs, rearranging clothes to fit into my pack, assessing my currency, checking for my passport and its copy, reviewing the timetables for the trains, and making sure I gave myself ample time to arrive at the station.

In most stations that I had encountered over the past few weeks, mishaps of one sort or another seemed unavoidable. On the one hand, train stations were an unsatisfying and mundane experience. On the other, they proved pleasant and relaxing. Much of the action took place there, and there is where someone like me might meet bevies of amenable female travelers who had also been backpacking for two or three months.

The more I thought about it, the less awful it seemed. For one, my Euro-Rail pass entitled me to first-class accommodations. It created a haven on wheels.

Membership has its privileges.

The weather, though, left much to be desired. However, if one was lucky enough to stumble upon a *bonne vivante*, then a rainy day could burst into sun-filled summer madness.

It is now 8 A.M., and I have just arrived at Central Station. I approach the ticket counter to pay my unwanted tariff. Tariffs were the downside of traveling by rail. For every country I visited by rail, I had to pay a travel commission fee.

"Good morning, mademoiselle," I said.

"Good morning to you, sir. How can I help you?" perked the station agent.

"I'm on my way to Frankfurt, Germany, and I need to purchase a ticket."

"No problem. That will cost you 20 guilders."

"I think I can handle that."

"Did you enjoy your stay here in Amsterdam?" she asked.

"Indeed, indeed, I did. You have a very lovely city. I expect to come back sometime soon," I stated with grandiloquent smiles.

"Well, have a safe journey to Germany."

"Thank you!" I said.

My ticket was first-class, direct to Frankfurt, with an open connection to Kassel. Again, I was excited and nervous at the same time. With each new embarkation, my stomach became squeamish.

I sat in Central Station for about ninety minutes. I read a couple of magazines and wrote in my journal. I was thinking how essential this visit to Germany would be for me, as I had preconceived notions about Germans and their history. Still, I pried myself open to whatever experiences would befall me. Just as I finished writing in my journal, I looked up at the schedule board and noticed that it was 10:15, and my train would leave in fifteen minutes from platform C.

The train arrived on time. I lifted my green, oversized pack, and prepared my ticket for entrance. Maneuvering through four train compartments, I made my way to first-class. I placed my pack in the overhead rest, and took a seat next to an olive-toned woman, with hair darker than midnight, deep, cola-colored eyes, an angelic aura, and a body by Fisher.

Of course, I was very pleased to see her, but I did not want to draw any attention to myself. Summoning my inner calm, I made myself as comfortable and as inconspicuous as I could. The ride would take five hours, and I did not want to make a scene.

Two months in Europe had taught me that anything was possible, and that every moment was an adventure. Europeans had a certain attitude about life and the moments therein. For them, life was enjoyed and appreciated in ways unfamiliar to most Americans. Life in Europe was lived with a freedom strange to me.

But, thinking of this freedom taxed my inner calm. How could I sit here next to this woman and not say anything? To remain silent would amount to being a slave. Is she single and available? If so, is she amenable? These questions formed a tidal wave battering my calm.

I decided to distract myself by placing a call to Hansel, informing him that I was on the 10:30 Mach train headed to Frankfurt, and that I would arrive in Kassel in approximately five hours, collisions notwithstanding. Repeatedly, I called, but no one answered. I left several detailed messages concerning my arrival, my whereabouts, and a precise description of myself, down to my gray flannels, Egyptian cotton broadcloth shirt, and cognac brogues.

I hung up the phone and headed for my seat. On my return, I noticed that she was gone. It was just my luck. Sitting down, I tried to suspend belief in her disappearance. Five minutes next to a black man from America, and she got scared and ran. Maybe my own insecurities and assumptions allowed me to think as much. But before I could relax, a subtle, sultry, thickly accented, elegant voice whispered in my direction. My heart raced like a greyhound in the bend at fifty miles per hour.

"Excuse me. May I have my seat?"

"Certainly, no problem . . . Let me get up . . . Here you are!"

I was glad to see her, and knew that I would say something before too long. But I decided to wait. I was hoping that she would initiate conversation. Patiently, I observed, spying for any an opportunity to engage her.

Eventually, I became weary of playing cat to her mouse. So, I pulled out my travel journal, flipping to my latest page. I skipped to a blank page and began a new chapter. It was precisely then that I felt a subtle change in her energy and presence. At the very moment that I had begun the new chapter, aptly titled, "Germany: Another Foreign Land Awaits," she turned slightly to her right, looking over her shoulder, her eyes following my hand as it traversed the page. She cleared her throat. I waited, thinking that, if she failed to say anything now, then she never would. I continued to write.

I felt as though she was rolling up an opinion about me and that this opinion was gaining momentum in her mind. Her mind seesawed. I believed that she wanted to ask me a question, but did not know where to begin.

I continued to write. I wondered if my focus on the journal was an aphrodisiac for her. Her opinion trembled, then suddenly avalanched out of control, forcing open her mouth. I continued to write.

The first one came tentatively, a light-winged fledgling. The others shot like falcons attacking prey or balls of cannon. But I ignored all of them. The more she asked, the faster my pen rolled. I sensed her energy heightening, yet there was no sign of anger or annoyance. I would eventually stop writing, but not yet.

I wrote of everything surrounding me: the syncopated click of the track, the beauty of the countryside, the wonder of the Rhone, the castles nestled on top of hills, their crowns barely protruding through the emerald canopy. I even recorded the variegated conversations prattling about the train. The glare of her eyes warmed my skin. She sat like a stolid scholar. She studied me in creative mode. She witnessed my mind at work, translating internal and external scenes into ciphers.

Alas, I emerged from the inter-zone. Were it not for the fact that I had even jotted down some of her questions, I would have forgotten them. Turning to my left, I was ready to talk. The questions were always the same. What is your name? Where are you from? How long have you been traveling in Europe? What do you do for a living? Where are you going to visit in Germany?

Inasmuch as my name appeared on the first page of my journal, I flipped there to silently answer her first question. She was sharp and observant.

"So, hello Anthony. How are you?" Curiosity painted her smile.

"I'm well, and sorry for ignoring your questions. But when I get into a zone, I can't respond to anything around me, can't break my flow. I become like a musician lost in a solo, visibly present but gone."

"What do you write about?" she asked.

"I write about many things. I especially enjoy writing poetry. Prose and fantasy, too. Whatever inspires me, I guess . . . I didn't get your name," I added in polite afterthought.

"My name is Jonquil."

"Jonquil is a beautiful name. Where are you from, Jonquil?"

"From Corsica."

"You're a long way from home. What brings you to Germany?"

"I am on holiday, and I have friends who live in Munich. I am going there for a week's vacation."

"It sounds like you're in for a terrific holiday. I wish you a good time."

"Where are you going, Anthony?"

"I'm on my way to Kassel; I have a friend there. This will be my first time in Germany. I'm looking forward to it." We searched each other's face, neither of us knowing what to say.

"So . . . you're from Corsica. I've never been there. I hear it's magnificent. I notice that only the wealthy go there."

"No, no, that's not true. All people come to visit the island."

For the first time, the ride had become rewarding. I reveled for awhile in the thought that someday I would cross paths with this woman again. Maybe not on this visit to Europe, but perhaps upon my future return. Now, I had a reason to take a trip to Corsica. Jonquil was definitely worth it.

I wanted to talk for the remainder of our ride, but sleep prodded me to nod. It would best to get her information now. E-mail would suffice. If meeting Jonquil presaged my stay in Kassel, then it would be a splendid trip indeed! Jonquil rejuvenated me.

"Jonquil, I am wondering if we can exchange information, I'd like to keep in touch. Would you be willing? You would give me a reason to visit Corsica, you know?"

"I don't know if this is good idea, we hardly know each other. But I don't see why we can't exchange information."

"Then, it's done. Here are my particulars."

Like Valentines, we exchanged information. Then, I went to sleep. I must have slept for at least two, two and one-half hours. The train stopped and Jonquil softly tapped me on my right arm to wake me. We had arrived in Munich. Here, I was to disembark, and make a long trek through the station's underground tunnel, to find platform D.

Something about rushing to make my connecting train en route to Frankfurt disconcerted me. Haste takes much out of the body. Of course, Jonquil's departure deflated me as well.

Before going our separate ways, I hugged her with a feeling of familiarity. I felt as if I had known her for ten years. It was a pleasure spending time with Jonquil on that short train ride. She was a cynosure amongst so many comely women from all around the world. If I were lucky, maybe I could meet someone precious like her while I continued my travel through Germany. These thoughts lifted me. Things felt right again.

The train station was hot, sticky, and filled with engine fumes. There were people everywhere, moving rapidly, hustling to make connecting rails. For a moment, I thought I was in New York's Grand Central Station.

Fortunately, the flow of passengers moved smoothly. Eventually, I found my way to platform D. Unfortunately, I noticed that one of my bags was missing. I had forgotten my toiletry kit. I needed that kit. It was packed with herb and other goodies I had purchased in Amsterdam. In less than twenty minutes, my train to Frankfurt would arrive.

If I ran, I could make it to the train from which I had just alighted, and back. So, I turned around and dashed through the underground. Before I could get a hundred yards into the tunnel, to my surprise, there was Jonquil walking quickly towards me with my black toiletry bag, smiling from cheek to cheek. I sighed a mountain, and consternation drained from my face quicker than quicksilver is quick.

"Jonquil, what's in your hand?" I joked. "That bag looks familiar," sweat dripped into my smile.

"I do believe this belongs to you!" she replied, gesturing.

"I believe that bag *does* belong to me. You're a lifesaver. Where would I be without you right now?"

"Oh, I don't know. You might be boarding a train to Kassel, I presume." She laughed and her bosoms shook like massive sugarplums.

"You're right about that! How could I possibly thank you? There is a God!"

"You can start by saying thank you and giving me a hug," she said playfully.

"I must say that you're an incredibly beautiful woman. I'm not saying this just because brought my kit."

"You think so?"

"Yes!"

"I'm doing what any other kind-hearted person would have done. It's okay. I have time before I meet my friends. I guess you can call it fate that brought us together a second time."

"Fate! I like that. Fate, bring me more fate like this!" my voice echoed in the tunnel.

"I know you have a train to catch, so you'd better be going."

"You're right. Would you mind walking with me over to platform D?"

"Sure, I think I can accommodate you, Anthony."

We walked to platform D talking and laughing. For a brief moment, I hovered far above the station. Again, that feeling of knowing her for years had overcome me. All I could think about was if and when I would see her after today.

As we approached the platform, I could see my train pulling into the station. I looked at her sadly smiling and wondering why there were no women like Jonquil back home. This woman had taken the time to find me in order to return my kit. I would love to see such thoughtfulness in stateside women. A beautiful woman doing what Jonquil had done was unheard of – at least to my experience.

Saddened that I could not spend more time with her, I thought about another hug. The train that would take me to Kassel had come to a stop.

"Jonquil, thank you again. You're wonderful. May I thank you *properly*?" I suggested.

"How might you thank me *properly*? Haven't you already done so?" she asked.

Slowly, calmly, I motioned for a hug. But before I could embrace her, she pulled me towards her and began kissing me. My mind could not wrap itself around this situation nor could I react quickly enough. 'Twas strange that she had read my mind. Even Fortuna must have been surprised.

I eagerly and hungrily welcomed her kiss. I wanted to feast on her soft, plush lips, but passengers were already boarding the train.

"Anthony, I wanted to give you something to remember me by. Thanks for sharing your art with me, and being such a gentleman. And yes...I am single. And I look forward to seeing you again. Maybe even while you are here in Germany."

Stunned, I stood there like an idiot in hardened cement, like a deer trapped in oncoming headlights. For a moment, all I could do was stare.

"Thank you. You've been a perfect lady. I'll look you up while I'm in Kassel. See you soon!"

"Goodbye Anthony! Until we meet again. *Au revoir, mon ami.*"

I walked away and proceeded to my train. Desperately I wanted to know what Jonquil was thinking. I never got an opportunity to tell her that I knew that she was named after a flower, *Narcissus jonquilla*. But I suspect that she knew as much anyway.

This ICE train is even nicer than the last one. There is a digital television with MPH built into my seat. This train is the terrestrial version of Virgin Atlantic planes with all of their high end amenities.

Settling into the last leg of my trip, I decided to watch some television. Turning on the TV, I see that *Fame*, the movie, is playing, starring Irene Cara and Debbie Allen. How much better could it get?

For the next week or so, I will not have any travel commission fees. I will take this time to learn more about the Germans and their history. I cannot believe that I am almost in Kassel. Is Mannheim the stop before Kassel?

My only concern now was whether Hansel had received my messages. I decided to place another call to him. I dialed the number. The phone rang continuously. No answer! I become paranoid. I called seven hours ago. Maybe Hansel is out of town; after all, he did tell me to call him on Saturday, or was it Friday?

Nevertheless, I am in Germany, and feeling edgy. To take my mind off of things, I pull out my journal and write a plea to God: "Lord, I pray to you and give you thanks for watching over me as I have journeyed throughout Europe beyond danger. I ask for your forgiveness, though I have sinned much on this trip. Lord, you know my heart. Keep your protection over me. Amen."

It is now 6:50 P.M., and I have been on the train since 10:30 this morning. We should arrive in Kassel in thirty minutes. I hope that Hansel will be at the station to meet me.

So far, Germany has been pleasant. The countryside is beautiful. The people have been rather friendly, and for some reason the women have been especially kind. On the way to the loo, a Fraulein group giggled out of their seats and fanned their hands as I passed the aisle. In the loo, I thought that, if Hansel is not at the station, I will have to take a train up to Switzerland and hang out there for a few days.

The train pulls into Kassel on time. I disembark with all of my belongings. I am ready to see Germany. But first, I must place another call to Hansel. I must also prepare myself for a trip to Switzerland or else back to Paris. Heading toward the phone booths, my stomach growls at me. My feet protest.

At Hansel's, there is still no answer. My mind stirs crazily. I did not come this far to miss my contact. My faith in people plummets. It hits rock bottom and seeks resurrection. I decide to wait around for an hour. If Hansel does not show by then, I will take the next train to Paris.

I calm myself and search for something to eat. Quickly, I learn how to say something in Germany besides *Danke schöen*, *Guten Tag*, and *Ist dieser Tisch frei?* I crave a chicken sandwich, but all I find is pork. Every part of the hog was for sale. I decide on a salad instead.

More than an hour passes, and still no sign of Hansel. After I finish my salad, I open my pack and pull out the train schedule. I search for the next train to Paris. There is one departing at 9:30. I am ready to bullet out of Germany.

As I am descending the ramp, en route to the platform, exhausted from a day of travel, disappointed by the absence of Hansel, like a gypsy appearing in thin air, a short, thin man is running up the ramp.

"Anthony! Anthony! Is that you? I'm Hansel, Ray's friend," he shouts.

"Hansel?"

"Anthony?"

"Yes, I'm Anthony. You're Hansel?"

"Yes! I'm sorry. I thought you were going to call me yesterday to tell me you were coming. I just got home and heard your voice on the answering machine, and drove here as fast as I could. How are you?" He huffs and he puffs.

"Much better now! What a relief! I was about to take another train, to Paris."

"Well, I'm glad you didn't. Let me take your pack."

"No, it's okay."

"I insist. You've had a long day. Allow me to help, please."

"Thank you, Hansel. You're too kind!"

"God is good," I say to myself. And Hansel's timing is right on time. My insecurities were beginning to display their ugly heads and my faith in people had taken a turn for the worst.

Hansel and I walked to his silver Volvo station wagon. The car looked new and comfortable. Hansel put my belongings into the car. We got in, and drove to his warehouse on the other side of town.

"Are you hungry, Anthony? Hansel asked.

"I could eat again. What did you have in mind?"

"How do you feel about Indian food?"

"Great. I love Indian food."

"Then it's settled. We eat Indian and then we go to a party afterwards."

"Sounds good to me. Thanks for showing up at the train station."

"Anthony, it is no problem. You are family. Let us take your things to my apartment, and then we go eat and party."

"*Wunderbar!*"

"I see you have already learned some German," Hansel added.

"*Ein bisschen*," I say.

Brothas Be

brothas be battling Babylon while
bomb shelling poison to da babies,
maybe they helped create lives at stake,
pushing and peddling drugs,
cuz thug is the mentality,
living pseudo-life styles, a dead man's reality
pimping a surrealistic paganistic devilish trip,
just to sip the "Amerikkkan Dream"
love Amerikkkan style enough to drive a "brotha"
wild.
dead and gone like a stillborn child.
mama didn't raise murderers, pushers, and pimps
to
span a generation of empty vessels,
hollow like a Columbus voyage.
dead Souls spreading death to young chocolate
souls,
hot like coal, fuckin' up many positive would-be
molds
silly ass simps, don't know that slavery is mental,
like an imp that pimps you to take negative actions
on
your own Black seeds, not knowing
you choppin' down lives like acres of weed
sold and smoked, as you choke, taking a toke to
make
your scrill screwing, the pill, she chills,
a baby born, and Babylon exalts the ills.
Tuskegee, Aids, Ebola...
brothas don't be knowin'

conspiracy is white supremacy.
I mean the point is to change the joint.
the joint of fast cars, fast women,
fast cash, fast ass, and fast lives
that don't make the night or dawn because
a mentality and respect for life is gone.
but brothas be knowin'
that the caged bird sings, behind bars, helping to create
more laws while the freed is scarred, soft and not hard, but pressed.
oppressed, depressed, suppressed, and hard-pressed to escape
babylon's chores
brotha's need to be knowin' that the end is near.
slavery is mental and there's much to fear.
It's past time, we need to change our minds
can't afford strange fruit
dangling from the vines of
estranged Black Thought. The price is too high
for Black Souls sold and bought.
How can heaven forgive us
If we slit our own throats?
If deadly conspiracies
dictate our reality
the inevitability is   our people's fatality.

Darkness

I arise from deep slumber, tainted
  with
    unwarranted mares stifling my ease.
      Comatose, I remain slippin' into
        peculiar darkness. Searching for a tangible
        solace... reaching...
        into Black Hole images
        amorphous.

Shapeless & eccentric, like minds of creatures
roaming Earth's pastures

      Unseen by my 3rd eye vision.
      I'm dizzy from academic missions
from...wishin' and fishin'...turnin' pages and
              seekin' sages...
                  my soul burns for
                    explanations, I yearn...
blood pressure rises and falls
      like Bay Area weather
      my search
          empty
            as I lie amorphous
          comatose
            slippin'
            into
              Black
              Hole
                spaces...

AMSTERDAM:
GROLSCH FOR TWO

Aunt Rachel had been planning a party for a few weeks now, and as luck would have it, I had freshly arrived from San Sebastián (Spain) on 11 July, just in time to partake in the festivities.

Eliza and I had just returned from a two-week trip to Spain, and we were about to part ways. For our last night together, we found a reasonable hotel. For our last night together, we stayed at Hôtel Utrillo on Rue Aristide Bruant in Montmartre. We brought in the morning with fireworks loud enough to elicit knocks of protest on the wall from the room next door. I was going to miss her. But what could I do? She had to get back to London, and I had to see my family. I was thankful for having met Eliza. She was a real jewel in Spain. Without her, I would have never made it through Spain. Eliza was a very special woman. I trusted that she would have a safe return to London, and eventually, to the States.

It was two days before Bastille Day (the French equivalent of America's Fourth of July). And if the latter was not enough, France had just won the World Cup over Brazil, the defending champions. Needless to say, pandemonium reigned in Paris.

Personally, I was hoping that the approach of Bastille Day would eclipse the World Cup hysteria. However, there was no such sign. Myriads of the French stormed the streets. For the first time, since the invention of the automobile, pedestrians were actually able to walk across the circle encompassing L'Arc de Triomphe: traffic had never stood so still. The Champs-Elysées was a bottle of champagne about to explode.

In every Métro station, the gendarmes prowled and patrolled. Outfitted in combat attire, toting semi-automatic weaponry, they were determined to keep the cork in place. On one hand, I felt safe. In retrospect, however, it was intimidating to witness the imminence of paramilitary (and even military force) ready to crush the head of civil disobedience. Suddenly, I could sympathize with world populations living under martial rule.

Today is 13 July, one day before Aunt Rachel's party and two days before I embark upon my journey to Amsterdam, where liquor, drugs, and carnality await me. At times, I wonder if I am ready to heed Dionysus' call? How different would Amsterdam be from Paris or from San Francisco for that matter?

Some small part of me harbored reservations, a much younger part that had been taught to eschew the pleasures of the world. But following the trip to Spain and my contortions with Eliza, I was ready to turn prodigal son, to tie my shoes tightly and to run through the streets of Tarshish.

The party started at 19:00. To my delight, I got to meet one of the original black American expatriates, Ted Joans, a poet of the fifties and sixties. Who would have thought that I would be at a party with Ted Joans, who rubbed elbows with Richard Wright, Chester Himes, Ollie "Bootsie" Harrington, Melvin Van Peebles, and others? I could not have imagined it.

For a woman who had only been in Paris for a short time, Aunt Rachel was rather well-known. I loved being at her place. You never knew who might walk through the door.

We were drinking, smoking, laughing, and eating Ronald's scrumptious barbecue. Provocative conversation abounded. One of Aunt Rachel's middle-aged friends was even trying to hit on me—the fact that she was married seemed not to matter to her. She had big, brown, enticing peepers, a raven pageboy, and a ripe, cinnamon kisser.

"What's your name?" she asked me, sitting down beside me on the sofa.

"Anthony, what's yours?"

"*Marguérite, enchantée.*"

"*Enchanté,*" I replied.

"Anthony, may I ask you question?"

"Depends on what it is."

"It's nothing compromising, I assure you."

"Then go ahead," I said.

"Do you know anything about computers?"

"I'm no Bill Gates, but I know a little."

"Then perhaps I might persuade you to come over to my place, and take a look at my PC."

"What's wrong with it?" I inquired.

"It overheats, darling."

I attributed it to Paris and liquor, French liquor, liquored Parisians. I gathered that I was twenty years younger than anyone else present. And I was drinking much less, too.

The next morning I was en route to Gare de Nord to catch the 7:30 train to Amsterdam. To say the least, I was dead tired. The Europeans with whom I had caroused seemed to survive without sleep. I did not blame them, but I had a hard time keeping pace.

At Gare du Nord, the queue for the train to Amsterdam seemed without end. People were literally camped out waiting for the train. I took many of the passengers to be Americans; AMERICA® was written on their faces. This was a good thing. I had forgotten my copy of *Let's Go Europe*. I had no clue about where to find a room, about what spots to hit in Amsterdam. I decided to tap the Americans for some inside dope.

"Hey, good morning! Where're you guys from?" I asked.

"From the States. I'm Kelly; this is Greg, Rob, and Emily."

"I'm Anthony. Pleased to meet you . . . Are you guys on your way to Amsterdam?"

"Yes, we are," Kelly replied.

"Cool, I guess we can all hang out together—if you don't mind."

"Sure, it's one big party with us, and we have room for one more person," Rob explained.

"I would appreciate it. Good looking out!"

"Anthony, do you know where you're going to stay?" Kelly asked.

"No, but I was hoping you guys could give me some information. Apparently, I left my *Lets Go Europe* on the métro, and I am pretty clueless about where to stay in Amsterdam."

"It's cool, Anthony. We have an eight-hour ride ahead of us. We'll all hang, get some brew, talk, and figure things out on the train. Don't sweat it, bro!" assured Greg.

"Alright," I said, "I'm cool with that. I'll see you on the train."

Across the station, I found a seat (not on the floor) and set down my pack. I leaned back, crossed my legs at the feet, and waited for the train to arrive. I had been in the station since 7:00 A.M. and it was now 8:30. I comforted myself by thinking of sleep on the train. I still could not believe that I was on my way to the city of sin, at least that is how I thought of it.

After another half-hour, a TGV pulled in, and we all made our way aboard. TGV stands for *Très Grande Vitesse* (Very Great Speed). There were comfortable-looking compartments with beds on the TGV. The train would reach Amsterdam via Belgium. Belgium was not a place I wanted to visit, knowing what Leopold and the Belgian army had done to Africans in the Congo.

Europe and America demanded rubber. At the turn of the century, the Congo was one of the world's few sources of supply. Leopold and his agents extorted labor from the native population, forced them to tap enough rubber trees to meet international quotas. A world of a darker hue perished trying to meet such demands under brutal conditions. Resources were ravaged and people virtually enslaved. A handsome income was drawn from the Congo. Leopold amassed an embarrassment of riches that would have made Midas mad.

Calling me from the other end of the car through which I happened to be passing was Kelly. I waited for her, Rob, Emily, and Greg to catch up. I settled for the room in which they would be riding. Though my ticket was first-class, I forewent a larger bed and more space in order to become familiar with my fellow Americans who would help me get settled in Amsterdam.

After thirty or so minutes of settling in, a French porter knocked on our door and requested our passports and reservations. I had noticed that there were many freeloaders on the trains of Europe. I had witnessed several passengers thrown off and apprehended by the authorities. The porter knocked again and entered.

"Pardon, messieurs et mademoiselles. J'ai besoin de vos passports et de vos reservations!"

"D'accord, pas de problème," we responded in unison, as we handed him our passports and proof of reservation. The porter inspected our documents, in turn, stamped them, and handed them back. We let out a collective sigh of relief. Although our papers were in order, every instant of having to show them produced momentary anxiety.

By now, we were all exhausted and ready for a nap. Kelly kindly offered me her headset. I accepted. She had noticed that I was cramped on the small bed. The bunk beds in coach were particularly narrow, designed for persons of wizened girth.

Nonetheless, the ride to Amsterdam proved nice and smooth. Though the lack of fresh air and the presence of five bodies in the smallish compartment gave me a touch of claustrophobia. But I set the volume of the headset at a relaxing level and fell asleep.

Eight hours later the TGV pulled into Central Station in Amsterdam, and we were still beat. Our priorities were the following: retrieving our packs, exchanging our currency, and making our way to a hostel.

We found the currency exchange, and turned francs and U.S. dollars into guilders. Next, we journeyed on foot to find the BA Hostel. Passersby gave us directions en route. As it turned out, the hostel was only about ten minutes from the station, which meant that we would be in the thick of the action. The next task, however, was to secure rooms for all five of us.

"Good evening. We're wondering if you have any rooms available," I asked.

"Yes we do, but I don't think we have enough rooms for everyone in your group. Did any of you make any reservations?" the receptionist asked.

"No, we didn't. We didn't know that we had to," Greg replied.

"Well, I'm awfully sorry. We're really busy during the summer months, and it is always best to call for reservations prior to arriving."

"What do you have available?" I asked.

"We have two spaces available for the women and two spaces for the men. But one person will have to wait to see if something becomes available."

"This puts us in a bit of a dilemma," Rob pleaded.

"I'm sorry, sir, but there's nothing that I can do at this time," the receptionist explained.

I figured that, inasmuch as I was not originally in this party, the only fair thing to do would be to let them have the available rooms, and to get a room elsewhere. Before I could inform everyone of my decision, a man in a gray herringbone sport coat, dungarees, no socks, and run-over loafers, smoking a cigarette in a holder, descended the main stairs. Pausing on the last step, he adjusted the fag, and headed toward the counter.

"Pardon me," he said to us, and stepped to the counter where he reached deep into his dungarees, pulling out a single key with no ring. He gently handed it to the receptionist, scrutinized us while puffing away, and left. The receptionist looked at us and said, "Welcome to Amsterdam!"

I was excited to be in Amsterdam. The good thing about being here was that, in addition to speaking Dutch, everyone spoke English and French as well. In some ways, Amsterdam was like being in London. Certainly, the weather here reminded me of London. The sky was a bowl of Pliocene soup. Amsterdam was London with a twist, but the people were nicer here and spoke with more of an American accent. Already, I liked Amsterdam.

My room was on the third floor: #325. Rob and Gene were my roommates. Whenever staying with strangers in a hostel or elsewhere, my *modus operandi* consisted of immediately questioning my roommates to ascertain their mindsets. So, I opened the door, greeted Rob and Gene, set my pack down, and fired away.

Later, I wanted to go down to the basement of the hostel. In the bathroom, I had overheard some students talking about the arcade, the television, the pool table, and the bar that was downstairs.

It was around ten and the night was just getting started. Though I was tired, I was not too tired to drink. As I made my way to the basement, I was comforted by the thought of Kelly, Rob, Greg, and Emily. They all had rooms on the second floor. We had plans to meet and gallivant at midnight. But besides tonight's plans, I was glad to know that at least a few people seemed to have my back.

Entering the basement, I was not surprised. I had seen such a room many times before. It was modeled in the style of a college dorm common room: Formica tables, bland tiles, faux wood paneling, and fluorescent lighting. But I was concerned less about the décor, and more about some cold bottles of Grolsch.

On the way to the bar, I glimpsed in my periphery the most gorgeous woman I had seen in Europe so far. Without hesitation, I sauntered to her table.

"Hello. How are you, sister?" I asked. Of course, I was making a huge assumption by calling her *sister*. In Europe just because she looks like me does not mean that she has had the so-called black experience. She might be offended.

"What's up, brother?" she replied.

"What's your name, baby? Where're you from?"

"My name is Teresa. I'm from New York, but I live in Paris. Where are *you* from?" she asked.

"Girl, I'm from Oakland."

"For real?" she cooed. "I have family in the Bay Area, in Berkeley, to be exact."

"Alright, momma! What're you drinking?" I asked.

"The same as you."

"You like Grolsch?"

"Sure."

"Solid!"

I ordered us two Grolsch and joined Teresa at her table. She had a flawless butterscotch complexion with features so soft that I wanted to reach out and caress them. Raven-black hair billowed up at her forehead and down to her shoulders like cirrus clouds. Her eyes shamed emeralds and topaz.

"Prost!" Teresa exclaimed.

"Prost!" I returned. "Here's to looking at you!"

"You'd like to, hunh?"

"Are you open to composing a memorable and tantalizing piece of art?"

"What do you have in mind?" I reluctantly replied.

"How about we compose a graphic and no holds barred display of literature that captures the mood of this decadent city? If you hadn't noticed, we are in the belly of the beast. We are in the heart of the red-light district, silly."

"Ok I am game. This will be a nice exercise of contrasting styles of writing and wit. Let's give it a whirl." I mentioned in slurred vigor.

Cinematic Inhibition

Standing on the threshold of precipitation
If I cross this line, my sense of
heaven/hell/pleasure/pain
Could become one enormous distortion of
compromise
The visuals are surreal, enticing, erotic, and alluring
It's a place that mama said, "Satan" lurks
It's everything a child of God is to avoid
Carnality is exploited to its highest degree.
It's Romanesque at its' microcosmic best
It's a scene that challenges the very nature of
morality
But who defines morality? Man? God? God's
words? Who?
Heaven is the pleasure one gets from simulated sex
acts, no penetration
Yet the body reacts
Pain is the extortion of one's financial budget
But the real pain is watching Satan in the form of
Dead Presidents being spent
To pleasure one's fleshy desires
I watch cautiously at flesh being used to survive
one's life styles
Back rooms of moans, gropes, and grunts,
Sounds are all you hear, as fantasies are
momentarily fulfilled
Egos are being catered to for the push of a
Jackson, Grant, or Benjamin
She tells them what they want to hear, she tells
him what he wants to hear

She tells me what I want to hear.
She whispers and echoes "big daddy, take your time, do me daddy"
"What are you working with?" $200.00 for it all.
$120.00 for a blowjob.
$80.00 for a hand job. She asks, "do you have a condom?"
She becomes a cinematic inhibition at a moment's notice for a few Dead Presidents
You cum for a price! There's the touch, the lick, the squeeze, the feel, the directions, the rules of engagement. She's directing the movie. Every whim, she controls. She's preparing for her next greatest performance, cause she smells the money, she feels the money, she sees the money. There is no play, before the pay.
You stick/move/play cat/mouse/you exchange for business sake
She teases / pleases / seizes / appeases / pushes /pull /in / out/ up /down/ over/ under-moving flexible like a gymnasts, every man's wildest fantasies being fulfilled at a moment's notices for a dollar, a frank, a guilder, or a pound.
She claims sticky wetness, hot and horny, but it's ego manipulation, verbal taunting
You can smell the perfume of sex in the air, and the rooms are private
Sometimes open
Guards, non-English speaking man the protect the doors from a distant
The rush of the thrill is addicting, it's like being hooked on a deadly substance (crack)

You can't release this demon unless you rehab for detoxing,
Unfortunately, there is no rehab for sexaholics,
It's the zenith of economic bargaining,

It's basic economics- supply and demand, you supply the money and she demands you cum. It's business, never personal. She proclaims, she is not a prostitute, a madam, or a call girl; but for the right price, when you call she'll be at your destination at a moment's notice. She says "it's a business and she is trying to make a living, but is tired of turning tricks. She will cut in a heartbeat to make that cash. This is fantasy, blissful surrealism. Who is she and what lurks behind those pretty brown eyes? What are her desires? Does she have goals for success in life, whatever that might be? I don't know, I never ask. Does she start her day as a waitress or student, becomes a stripper, an exotic dancer or a business woman at night? It's all for money, entertainment, and survival.

The Window: A Collaboration

Damn, all these people, another night another dollar. I wonder who's first? Is he coming over or not? Maybe someday I can stop all this hustling. How long can I maintain this lifestyle, this dead end work? Fuck men...I have a horrible love/hate relationship with them. Sometimes I wonder what life holds for me. Men must be sick to pay for a sex service. Maybe I'm the insane one to sell my body for money. It's a living...oh well! There's nothing else I can do but this pays the bills. I don't have an education, so, I must do this to survive. But I believe in the Cinderella fairytale. One day a man will walk into this parlor and see thru me. He'll look into my eyes and see me for the woman I am. He'll rescue me from this sinful life. He'll take care of me and I'll never have to be a part of this anymore. I'll be free or will I?

Will he really see me? Will I be stuck? Dave says he loves me; but does he? I am doing him freely, but everybody else pays. I never thought I'd ever be in this situation...hey he's a cutie...Where you going sugar...uh oh who the hell is this idiot...please keep walking. Could Dave ever truly love me? He says he does. He comes three times a week to be with me. Ugh, these tourists. Why are they always trying to snap photo? Grandpas gawking. I am so tired of it. I hear they have a play in NYC call "The Life." I think I'd love to check it out someday. A play based upon the oldest, but non-respected profession, who would have thought?

PARIS:
CAFÉ DE LA PAIX

Café de la Paix. 12 boulevard des Capucines, place de l'Opéra 75009 High-noon.

Eighty degrees of Fahrenheit. We are sitting toward the back, cater-corner to the main bar. Our silhouettes are camouflaged by shadows sired by the Sun King's idol. We luxuriate in high-back leather chairs with plush arms. Classical jazz softens the background. The place is really a dive for old money, a place where *old* means eighteenth or nineteenth century.

If you sit here long enough, you will see someone you know pass by, so the Parisians say. I suppose we are well placed. Café de la Paix is grandiose and fashionable, but the service is brusque, at best. The clientele is an anonymous mixture of business people and all-day shoppers. The coffee is fabulous, but the food is outrageously over-priced. I will not be eating much, perhaps a salad. As for wine, I will have as much as my body can hold, and that will be about a battleship.

We order a bottle from Alsace, intoxicatingly clear. The brother across from me is from New York. He has been in Paris since 1969. I was born in 1968. He tells me that he has experienced the "Golden Age."

"What was it like?" I prod him.

"You mean the 'Gollllllllllllllllllllllllllllllden Age.'"
Evidently, it must have been a paradise. Of course, I had heard stories about how black GI's, intellectuals, artists of all stripes,

especially musicians, had Paris tottering on its heels. *The Negro Review* electrocuted the Champs-Elysées.

"Yes, the 'Golden Age'," I said.

"I'm not talking about that," he snapped.

"You mean the change in the landscape," I suggested.

"Yes, that's right, the *decline* of an era." He stops, takes a long breath, lights a Gauloise, and begins to recount those halcyon days of his European bachelorhood.

"You know brotha, there was a time when a black man meant something here in Paris. We could pick up girls without the slightest effort." He leans back, and snaps his finger. A dazzling chocolate lady with marcelled hair in a cream-colored, two-button, wool gabardine suit moves across the café as if summoned by him. He looks at her, then at me. She looks at neither of us. His face crinkles with knowledge, or is it bewilderment, or should I say disappointment? Vaguely, for an instant, he resembles Ogotomeli sitting under a Baobob tree on a star-filled African evening. My interlocutor is a jazzy sage?

"Yes, brotha, it was the 'Gollllllllllllllllllllllllllden Age.'" I imagine mountains of decadence and seas of indulgence. The *garçon* finally brings our bottle. The sage gives him a king's ransom for a tip, and I bite my bottom lip in shock.

"The tip is key to your respect and existence, here," says the sage who suddenly seems a fool. I am thinking that he is from Saturn or Uranus because I cannot follow his reasoning. "How long has he been this way?" I wonder. *Chacun à soi*, the French say. *To each his own*, I recall, and continue to prod.

"What was the percentage?" I ask with renewed interest.

"You mean for the tip I left?"

"No, the *girls*. I want to know how much was out there."

"As I recall, there was boo-coo," he says.

"How much is *boo-coo*?"

"Boo-coo, brotha, boo-coo—"

"In the States, in Atlanta, for instance, they say the ratio is six to one. What was it when you first came here?"

"Like ten to one. For every brotha there was at least ten white girls. French ones, Belgian ones, Dutch ones, German ones, Swedish ones, Danish ones, Norwegian ones, Italian ones, Spanish ones, even, a few Russian ones. In smaller towns like Lyon and Marseilles, we were like kings of medieval dominions. Those were the good old days, a brotha had all the loving he could handle."

As he finishes, a rather tall gentleman approaches our table from the other side of the café. Gentlemen . . . "

"*Bonjour, mon ami,* " my interlocutor intones. "*Garçon, another round. This time, two bottles,*" he commands, snapping his fingers twice. The man who has joined us looks definitively

Mandingo, like Jack Johnson or anyone of his ancestors plucked from the Niani Coast.

This time, the *garçon* returns swift as Hermes, cradling a bottle in each forearm. The *garçon* presents the labels for inspection. My interlocutor nods, and the *garçon* uncorks them with ease. "*Un moment . . .*" the *garçon* trails off and returns with three new glasses. He sets two of them before Interlocutor and one in front of the stranger. He pours a jot in each for my interlocutor. The latter nods approvingly, and the *garçon* fills all of our glasses before trailing off again.

"How much have *we* had?" the stranger chuckles. I identify his accent as West Indian, but I cannot tell quite where.

"Only one," I volunteer.

"You can't fool me!" the stranger declares.

The stranger looks like Sandtop Licorice with a white streak accentuating his goatee. His bearing suggests that he has been around all of the *arrondissements* a few times.

"*How* many?" he asks again, impatience surging into his baritone voice.

"I don't understand," I finally admit.

My interlocutor breaks his smiling silence and intervenes. "He wants to know how many of those Golllllllllllllllllllllllllllllllden years you've spent in Paris."

"About eight," I say, lying to keep from being laughed at. Both of them laugh anyway, my interlocutor like a hyena, the stranger like a delirious locomotive full of rum-flavored coal.

"I've been here for over thirty years," boasts the stranger, "and alas, the well seems to be drying up. *C'est vrai.* After so many years here, you start to lose your edge. It's true. Just pay attention to the other brothers coming in and out. They look healthy and full to their eyes with—how do you American blacks say?—poo-see, but give them time. Theirs will turn to dust, too."

I wondered if the Golden Age had really dissipated or was I born into the wrong time period to cash in on the benefits of such a treasured era long gone. Obviously, these men had grandiose tales to spout, how believable were their stories, only heaven knows. One thing for certain, is, if you stayed in Paris long enough and made your rounds to popular waterholes, chances are you might luck up on many of these surreal storybook escapades, known discretely as the Golden Age.

These pretentious conversations were merely languid trophy stories of yester-years. It was funny not to be indulged of stories regarding the triumphs for African-American artistic and political dignitaries. As we belabored, and I continue to listen to these gentlemen rant, I longed to be engaged more about the Parisian Black Harlem Renaissance; and places like Le Grand Duc, one of the most popular night clubs of Montmartre. I needed to hear of the famous Hotel Liseaux, where Langston Hughes would stay. My senses carved to feel the spirit of Boulevard de Clichy, and the terrific tales of the butte (knoll), referred to as Montmartre.

More peculiarly, I marveled at the notion that, not one mention was made of the famed Le Fouquet Restaurant on the Champs-Elysees, a famous social meeting ground, where the likes of Gordon Parks, Richard Wright, and James Baldwin would frequent. For me to inquire about these historic curiosities; while these gentlemen reminisced so passionately on their multitude of European female conquests would have seem out of line, so I respectfully restrained my tongue.

A part of me wondered what Golden Age was I privy to in this conversation? I guess it was a treasured desire not to be caught in the snarls of segregation for these men. Paris was an honest, open oasis, an expression of freedom for them. I instinctively knew, that these escapades were not a normality for these me in the States in their times. Being conscientious of the complexion of miscegenation back home, I knew, what outcomes of such tales would have befallen them, had any acted on their constrained inhibitions Stateside.

So many told and untold tales casually combed my brain, as I sat, drank, and listened to the wisdom of my interlocutors. If I could have traveled back in time with H.G. Wells, and landed in Parisian cultural sobriety; dabbling in Jazz, listening to Sidney Bechet "Petite Fleurs," drinking wine, strolling Montparnasse, writing novels, prose, sonnets, essays, discussing global politics, at Café Monaco, watching a tantalizing Josephine Baker perform her famed banana dances, half-cladly dressed, catching a Duke Ellington show, meeting a young Melvin Van Peebles, and hob-knobbing with a youthful Quincy Jones; I believe this is where my spirit would have lighted.

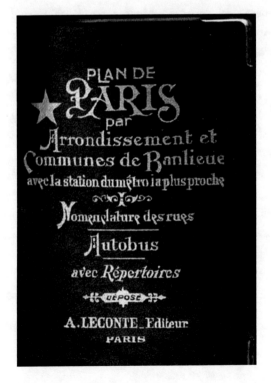

Paris: Place de l'Opera

I am in Baldwin's heaven.
Sipping on wine, people watching,
and making entries in my journal
A busy mid-summer breezy August evening, calm,
serene.
I come here to relax, to shop, exchange currency
at
Le Banc de Lebonais
I get the best exchange rates there (a best kept
secret).
My spirit is overwhelmed with the pulse of this
city and
the beauty it displays.
I am addicted to the street ambiance, enthralled by
its
pristine illumination
Architecture designs. I have fallen in love once again.
Paris, you are my muse.
I sit here in the (9th arrondissement, the right
bank),
an area around the Opera Ganier.
I sit amidst the capital's densest, concentrated by
both
department stores and offices.
I am centered, elevating, inhaling, and loving the
smell
of the city streets, Place de l'Opera.

Pain Au Raisin

I awake early every morning, gently greeted by Ra's beams
I stumble, making my way à la salle de bains pour se laver.
Finally, coherence caresses my skin, the morning bursting with opportunity
My mouth waters, salivating with anticipation of my favorite breakfast, un jus d'orange et un pain au raisin.
I make my way to le Metro at Pont de Neuilly once again to momentarily experience a fast past subterranean life, as I descend the stairwell.

PARIS:
CLUB ATLANTIS

Rue de Château. It is Saturday 12:14 A.M. I leave my hotel and head northwest toward the Métro at Pont de Neuilly, two stops before La Défense. Cafés, banks, and investment companies comprise the visible symbols of wealth in these Parisian outskirts.

The night is clear with a touch of crisp. Across distances, lights from the Eiffel Tower flatter the city, conspicuously, ever so proudly like a bright-eyed peacock spreading lapis lazuli and jade before zealous onlookers.

I walk three long Parisian blocks before I arrive at Métro Pont de Neuilly. I descend lonely stairs into a warm and steamy subterranean world where young and old, alike, sport festive attire, hungry for the carnal and bewitching moods of nighttide.

I remove my Carte d'Orange from my inside coat pocket, place the pass into the turnstile, and proceed to the station platform. My destination is Club Atlantis. In five minutes, the train arrives.

Entering, I take a seat nearest the double doors. After seven minutes of travel, I alight at Bastille. I walk to another platform, hoping that I did not miss my connecting train to Gare d'Austerlitz.

Fortunately, I make it. The train should arrive at Gare d'Austerlitz in ten minutes. It does so without incident. I leave the station and walk five blocks south, passing Bullet Trains still asleep, ganglia of train tracks, and aged, stoic warehouses with cataracts for eyes, before arriving at Club Atlantis.

"*Bonsoir*," chimes the host at the entrance, as he extends a courteous hand.

"*Bonsoir*," I reply, forgetting that I am in Paris.

At the ticket window, a ravishing woman of African descent is collecting francs. She has a mouth that makes me want to become a lifetime kisser. "Debit or cash?" she asks in French. I pay with paper francs.

The ambience was strange, or maybe just unique. The scene was dark, weighted with heavy smoke. A chiaroscuro sea moved across the dance floor. Afro-Parisian, Euro-b-boy, and an occasional dashiki formed the fashion. So did Frenchified blacks looking down their broad noses.

I spotted snow bunnies but not Trish, Terry, and Ronnie, my American friends experimenting with the expatriate life. If they were on the dance floor, then I could not see them. On the way to the bathroom, I found them tucked away in an alcove along the back corridor.

"I've been looking everywhere for you guys," I protested.

"We've been waiting for you right *here*, for over an hour," they retaliated.

"How am I supposed to see you back here?" I sighed grandly. "Look, Ronnie—" then I turned abruptly.

The bathroom was as filthy as any bathroom in an American club. Why did I think it would be different in Paris? Romantic notions of Paris did not make this crapper any less disgusting. What made it worse, it was so small you could hardly take a piss. Obviously, the architects of this water closet (as the French call the toilet) did not have my gene pool in mind. Momentarily, I appreciated America and its conception of *large* places in which to discharge. The same was true of the French shower or *douche*: too damn small.

As I am relieving myself, I begin to overhear a conversation spoken completely in French. To my surprise, I understand all of it. But then, I recalled that Africans spoke French with less rapidity and arrogance than white Parisians.

The conversation grew louder.

Senegalese: "One must be quick and clever in dealing with these women. Or, one becomes prey for the next vulture."

Malian: "Is *that* how it is?"

Senegalese: "They come here to get the black experience. It's our duty to give then a taste of chocolate."

Malian: "What is this chocolate you are referring to?"

Senegalese: "Look, get off of that high horse. I'm here to have a good time. Did you come here to get laid or not? You're here to *craque-craque*, right? Correct me if I am wrong, brother."

Malian: "But I'm tired of white women?"

Senegalese: "What else is there? Il y a seulement des femmes blanches. Vous comprenez?"

On the dance floor, bodies flail in a chocolate-ivory tsunami. Pallid teeth flash like Wodabbae smiles for Mauritanian brides. Socca, reggae, hip-hop, calypso, and Brazilian beats stir the waves. Skin-friction-electric46-copulation shocks even the wallflowers.

Upon my return, Ronnie introduces me to several of those whom I would call *groupies* looking for a weekend pass to the Id of Negroid.

"This is my friend visiting from the States," Ronnie projects. They all smile like anthropologists.

"What's your profession?" asks one of them. Her name is Snow.

"I'm a teacher and writer," I reply.

"So . . . you write. What do you write?"

"Fiction, poetry, fantasies, but mostly about castles in the sky."

"What kinds?" she pushed me.

"All kinds," my smile insinuated.

"How good are you?"

"Good enough to get to Paris."

The other women marvel at the tsunami, but my presence seems to distract them. Moments later, they eyed me with questions.

"I contemplate my experiences from inside a black and white fish bowl. I'm interested in black-white coexistence," I prepare to tell them.

"What do you mean?"

"There's still much controversy in the States surrounding the mixing of black and white," I would explain.

"What's the problem with black and white mixing?"

"The fear of the black penis. White men think we're going to help birth the whole world brown. They prefer economic competition to sexual competition.

Consider the dance floor. What white man can thrive in that tsunami? Perhaps a few. Maybe Tom Jones, in his youth."

The music becomes slow and sticky. The air billows thick with cannabis swirls that entice my unsuspecting lungs.

"Do you want to dance?" she asks.

Without hesitation, I grab her by the arm and we rush to the dance floor. It is swollen with heat and sweat. The dance floor has spawned an amorphous organism out of its sea. It wears perfume and cologne and shaves its armpits. It uses fluoride toothpaste, but deodorant without aluminum.

I feel her thighs and breasts pressing against me. I hear no words. I taste salty attraction. We sock the socca. Sweat drenches the sound. We are still floating. Her eyes are closed, but mouth open as if swallowing erotic juices.

Back at the table, she lights into me.

"Your hypothesis about sexuality is fallacious."

"You're entitled to your opinion."
"I believe I am."

"Do you believe in myths?" I ask.

"What?"

"Do black men have tails?"

"Are you being funny?" she asks.

"During WWII, a rumor began circulating throughout France that black men had tails. And white women went crazy over this myth. They wanted to know how long these tails were."

"Some myth!" she snorted.

"Do you believe it?"

"Believe what?" her annoyance said.

"Do you believe that sexuality is equality?"

"Yes."

"If a white man sleeps with a white woman. And if a black man sleeps with a white woman, is the black man therefore equal to the white man?"

"Yes."

"Is sexual freedom a viable substitute for economic freedom?"

"It might be. What does it matter anyway? You worry too much."

Before I can set the record straight, Ronnie comes over to the table to tell me that someone wants to meet me.

"This woman is really digging you," insists Ronnie. "She looks like she wants to eat you along with her baguette and brie."

"Why me?" I connive.

"She thinks you are some American celebrity. She asked me if you were a rap star."

"Why not a rap producer?"

"How's that? Look, there she is."

"I think I'll pass."

"Stop being so cynical, come over to the table and meet her."

"Okay, but let me order a drink first." I smile wryly at Snow, and she returns the compliment, flinging her tresses. I take the long way to the bar. Once I get there, it takes me five minutes trying to explain to the bartender that I want a Pierre Ferand floater in a glass of Veuve. Alas, the drink. I leave a fair tip and take the short way to their table.

"*Bonsoir.*"

"*Bonsoir,*" greets the table.

Immediately, I am impressed by her straightforward calm.

"How are you?" I direct toward her.

"Fine. How are you?""

Reggae answers a question with a question, "*Voulez-vous danser avec moi?*"

"Yes."

"*Allons-y ! »*

She does not press her thighs and breasts against me, yet I feel her. The reggae eventually gives way to Parisian hip-hop. She reads my face.

"Don't you like this song?"

"No."

"I'm thirsty anyway. Let's get something to drink," she offers. At the bar, we begin talking. At the bar, we get cozy. She brushes away one of her bangs before ordering Johnny Walker Red. This time, I order chartreuse.

"How do you gain your bread?" I ask.

"I'm a student."

"Really."

"Yes."

"What's new at the university?"

"James Baldwin."

"What?" I'm shocked.

"Yes. A retired French professor who taught English literature in America is teaching an entire course on James Baldwin."

"What are you reading?"

"Right now, we're reading *Notes of a Native Son* and *The Price of the Ticket* . . . Have you read them?"

"Several times. First, when I was ten."

"Really."

"*Mais oui.*"

We finish our drinks, and she invites me back to her flat for cappuccino. I accept.

Returning to their table to get my leather, Ronnie asks, "Are you leaving with her?"

"I'll see you later. Paris is calling."

"Snow left in a huff. She says you stopped talking to her because you didn't agree with everything she said."

"Please tell her that she will be sorely missed."

"Now, you're being sarcastic. She seemed really into you."

"You don't say."

"Really . . . she told me, all teary-eyed, that you misunderstood her."

"How so?"

"She said that you thought she was a negrophile."

"A negrophile? Maybe Snow is just looking for her fifteen minutes of fame."

"Anthony, are you serious?"

"Yes, Ronnie. Look, I gotta go."

"What should I tell Snow?"

"Tell her to look me up during the next golden age."

"What are you talking about?"

"Ask me tomorrow morning."

We Loved

We love-morning, noon, and night
I know the nocturnes of your ways
I know your place of passion and pleasure
I see the "Spanish Apartment" in your eyes
I see Villas, beaches, and strolls on island antiquity in
spirit
I understand the Dream
Hopeless romantics resolved
They come to terms, when loved
Come fly with me and let me taste
The nectar of your love

Your Spirit Found

Like an oasis in a desert your spirit found me
Like a Spanish Bolero in triple meter you loved
me
Like Jamaican rain your kisses caressed the brown
of my skin
Parisian moonlights are timeless as you
Mind's eye sees you as an ancient world wonder,
wonderfully, wondrous
Divinity manifests creation on Earth inside you
Spirit of yours found
Your spirit found
Your spirit found
Spirit of yours found
Love me on Cypress shores
Swim with me in Sardinian lagoons
Stroll with me under an Andalusia illumination
Feel my spirit underneath you,
Like an oasis in the desert we found, balance

SPAIN:
BEYOND THE BEGINNING

Aurora will spread her rosy fingertips soon enough. And when she does, I will be en route to Barcelona-Sants, the central rail station in this archaic and magnificent city.

There, I will purchase a ticket, pay a tariff, and wait in a line that trails to infinity. Clutching a paper number, I will vacillate between vexation and anticipation, before an irritable clerk (who does not speak English) summons me. I will communicate as best I can, and if I am successful, I will have finally secured my passage to Granada.

Yet rosy-fingered dawn is nowhere to be seen, and I will deal with her and all that she brings at the appointed hour. But tonight, my last night in Barcelona, life is to be lived, so I hop bars with David deep into crepuscular hours.

Barcelona is an aphrodisiac. Everything about this city exudes love and romance. Seduction confronts you, open, waiting to be embraced. Bolero music, sangria, humidity, beaches, and voluptuous women of Mediterranean visage conspire to make a man cream his pants. Barcelona is an ancient paradise engulfed in gaudy, lavish decadence. Paris is supposed to be so romantic, but Barcelona far surpasses it. The balmy weather, the overt nudity, and the appreciation of bodily desire define Barcelona. (I have forgotten all about the garbage and fish smell).

Embarking upon the night with David, I became sentimental and teary-eyed. Barcelona was just beginning to sway me and I was not ready for it to stop; its promise seemed great.

I had learned the Metro, had seen the Sagrada Familia, toured the Picasso Museum. I had shopped along the famous Las Ramblas, strolled La Ribera, idled in the Garcia district, mingled with students worldwide in Plaza del Sol, spent innumerable hours at Plaza de España, in awestruck gaze of the lights of the Magic Fountains. I had contemplated Gaudi's masterpieces and walked the entire length of Diagonal, the main thoroughfare. But through all of this, I had not learned almost no Spanish. Still, I managed to get by.

"Anthony, are you okay?" David asked.

"Yeah, I'm cool. Just feeling a little blue. That's all."

"You sure?"

"Yeah. Let's do this!" I said, summoning my strength.

"So no regrets! It's all about the ride. Take the ride!" David advised, brotherly.

"I guess you're right. The rest of Spain awaits me. Barcelona is just a piece of the pie, a snapshot among many. Bring on the drinks and the señoritas, señoras, tambien!" I declared.

"Let's hit the strip first. Then, we'll swing by Jamboree, and see what happens from there. I know you have to leave tomorrow, so we won't keep you out too late."

"Look, D., I'm cool, really. No sleep for me tonight. I'll sleep on the train. Besides, I get insomnia before every departure."

We walked over to Las Ramblas to see what the strip had to offer. With drinks in hands, we strolled for over an hour, but found nothing to our liking. Having drained two six-packs, we made a beeline to Jamboree. The Jamboree is a watered-down version of a San Francisco hip-hop club. The Jamboree's biggest attraction is that it is multi-ethnic. Its biggest drawback is the music: a one-sided version of hip-hop, so-called gangster à la L.A. and Long Beach. Apparently, the DJ's had never heard of the Native Tongue school.

Here, I saw the imitation of American life. Spanish kids emulated American mannerisms of cool. They wore black American hip-hop attire, fashion for the streets. Jet-black Senegalese and Gambians, dressed like black Brooklynites, gesticulated like West Coast players, and held seas of Spanish girls enthralled. I saw the culture I had grown up in, my culture mimicked by Spaniards and Africans alike. I was both disgusted and intrigued.

The crowd at Jamboree had no real understanding of black, urban life in America. They had superficially adopted an exported model of blackness, of hipness. I felt that my swagger was being compromised. Where did cultural borrowing end and exploitation begin? What were the consequences of misrepresenting another culture? And what could I do here in the midst of all of it? To my surprise, this cultural impersonation annoyed even David, an Italian American by way of San Jose (California).
"Anthony, these people think they're from the 'hood," he confided."

Immediately inside the entrance to Jamboree, a stairwell spirals to the basement, which is really a quarry. Iridescent strobe lights color clouds of smoke. Doric columns pierce the clouds. Bedrock doors conceal private rooms. Mini-bars project asymmetrically from the walls. Bouncers keep mobile vigil. Though it is summer, coolness fans the room.

David and I ascended the staircase to the top floor. By now, both of us wanted to dance, but neither of us could speak a lick of Spanish. How were we going to ask anyone to dance without seeming featherbrained or desperate? We did not know, so we decided to get our jag on, instead.

In a corner, behind the bar, next to a couple of Asian girls, we spotted three Arabs smoking hashish. Here was our chance, my last night in Barcelona. We sauntered over hesitantly.

"Are you sure about this?" I asked David.

"I'm game; no fear, remember?"

"Excuse us," David said, "but we're trying to score some hash."

"We have some," said the man sporting a mandarin orange, short-sleeve silk shirt. "Eighty pesetas."

To our surprise, not only did the Arab speak perfect English, but he was direct and to the point as well. David fished some bills out of his pocket, counted them, and handed the man his price. The man handed David the hash wrapped tightly in cellophane. David put the hash in his pants pocket, and we walked to the bar.

"Allow me to get the first couple of rounds," I said.

"Why is that?" challenged David.

"You got the smoke, after all."

"Of course. You're leaving tomorrow. Consider it a going-away present."

"Alright, but I'll get the drinks."
"Okay," David conceded.

In English, I ordered four Heinekens. "Veinte pesetas," demanded the bartender. Placing the pesetas on the counter, I said, "Here you go, amigo." By the time the Heinekens arrived, David had already fired up. I turned to see him bending down, between his knees, coughing. "Must be the chronic," I thought to myself.

When I turned again to give David his beers, he was nowhere to be found. I scanned the bar, then the dance floor. He was grinding against a stunningly attractive Spanish mommy.

Cradling all four beers, I squeezed through the crowd, dousing people, and handed two bottles to David. He offered one to mommy, and she smiled gratitude. I turned to leave, but David grabbed me by the shoulder. Hash was in his hand and a psychedelically colored glass pipe. I set one of my beers between my feet, and placed the goods in my back pocket. Downstairs, in the coolness of the cave, I smoked heavenly. Then, I returned upstairs and danced with nine or ten women. I figured out that all I had to say was *bailar* and point to the dance floor. The hash permitted me to move like Bojangles, but none of the women held my attention.

At 5 A.M., I found David in the basement sipping dark liquor. I motioned for us to go; my train departed in three hours. We walked to David's hotel, located about three blocks from mine just off Las Ramblas. Seeing David through the door, I said good-bye and left. As I was walking down the street, I heard David yelling voluminously.

"Anthony don't lose my number, I'll hook up with you in a few weeks in Paris. E-mail me!"

"Get some rest, David. I'll call you," I shouted back. He leaned forward like a broken question mark, staring down the street. My guess is that he could not keep me in focus. The next time I turned around, he was gone.

Back at my hotel, I took a cold shower, a short nap, and began to pack. Excited at the prospect of finally visiting Granada, I finished in what seemed like no time.

I could not believe that I would soon be in Granada, the former capital of the caliphate, the stronghold of the Moors in Spain.

I would visit Alhambra and run my fingers over the delicate arabesques carved on its walls. The breeze sweeping down from the Sierra Nevada would refresh me, giving me the strength of Tarik and seven thousand Africans landing at Mons Calpe and overthrowing the Gothic kingdom of Spain. I finished packing, put my papers in order, and bounded down three flights of stairs to the concierge's desk. I handed over my keys, and proceeded to Barcelona-Sants.

The train station was twenty minutes away by Metro, and I could have walked there, but I was dead tired. Instead, I walked back up Las Ramblas to the Catalunya station.

The train arrived in about fifteen minutes. I boarded and took a seat closest to the double doors. I noticed dozens of people with packs like mine, no doubt, headed to the station as well. The ride was speedy and without incident: not one gypsy or panhandler accosted me. Consequently, I was able to rest a little.

At Barcelona-Sants, about a dozen of us packers alighted. This station was calm and the air lethargic compared to those of Paris and of London. Rumor had it that the Spanish rails were the worst, and I soon found out that said rumor was not a rumor.

I hesitated about going to the window to purchase my ticket. I neither spoke nor understood Spanish. Neither had I heard any English at all in the station.

On my way to the window, I reached into my pack to retrieve my wallet. I intended to pay for my ticket with a credit card. Looking up, I saw the clerk behind the window waving me off, pointing vigorously in the direction from which I just come. Boiling water was not hotter than I.

I turned to see a number machine. I looked back at the clerk to ascertain where he had been pointing. He shook his head in affirmation. I walked back to the machine and took a number. A wave of paranoia crashed over me; my ticket read 150. Every hotel in Barcelona was booked; I could not stay another night. The room I had come as a result of a German's generosity: Jürgen had given me the key and let me stay there for half price until his friends returned from Rome. They were due back this morning.

The train was scheduled to depart at 8:00 A.M. and the station clock said 7:45. It did not seem like there were one hundred and fifty people ahead of me; I suspected that some had become tired and left.

I waited and waited. Then, I waited some more. And after waiting, I waited again. The clock now said 8:00. I was going to miss the train to Granada. To my surprise, an announcement came over the PA. I did not understand what I heard, but gathered from people's expression that the train had been delayed. Then, the schedule board confirmed as much. I was pissed.

The clock said 8:30 when I finally got to the window. When I placed my credit card on the counter, the clerk looked me and shook his head.

"Sir, I want to buy a ticket to Granada and I want to pay with this card," I said in English.

"*No tarjeta de crédito,*" he replied.

"I want to pay with credit," I repeated.

The clerk looked at me with disturbed countenance.

"*No tarjeta de crédito,*" he hissed again. What was wrong with my card? "It's as good as anyone else's," I murmured to myself. I was not over my limit. I could have sworn that other passengers had paid with plastic. I wondered if Jim Crow spoke Spanish.

Resorting to hand gestures, I tried to explain once again that I wanted to pay for my ticket with the card. Again, the agent looked at me, sternly. "*Solamente dinero. No tarjeta de crédito...negro-*"

The last word rang clear. I did not bother to listen for what followed. I could read faces. I had cleared my throat to spit, but stopped before I opened my mouth. I looked back at the clerk with assault in my eyes.

What else could I do? I wished I knew Spanish: I wanted to tell the clerk a few things. Pulling out cash, I slammed it on the counter, snatched my ticket and went to find a seat. Unfortunately, all of the first-class tickets had been sold out.

At 9:00, I boarded the train for Granada.

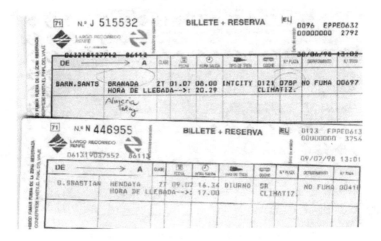

Revolutionary Erotica

My phallic point spills wetness all over this page
Every drop takes a new direction in pointillism,
artistic surrealism
Each drop creates a different sensation,
Touch, taste, smell, sight, sounds ticking the senses
Like honey from my scepter
We are the Tantra of past/present times
Revolution is the way we create love, eternally
Inhibitions rendered freely
Liberation sexing outside the box of normality
Bodies of silhouetted images
Human clay, Earth!
God's first Adam and Eve, spiritually human, not
divine
Exiting sheltered warmth from isolation,
Stimulation, galvanization, tantalization
Stepping into cosmic paradise, rolling their carnal
dice
Naked, baptized by heaven's tears
I sculpt you with lyrical clay
You manifest, acquiesce, and evanesce
Time becomes ancient recollections
I cannot decipher romantic Sanskrit, but I
understand my personal love script
Love's revelations, mysterious taboos, world's
unknown, indifference
Straddling the fences between Afro/Euro
sensibility
Duality, duplicity, dichotomy, multiplicities
Complicity of complexities, invisible destinies

Patience is patience
And my nature is complex, perplexed, compelling,
next, next, next...
Traveling cultural odysseys
Reflection of a soul's rebirth, terse
What is my worth? What is my value? I am a
metaphoric Black Stallion
Loving the sexual drug, the high, the bliss-never
dismissed
Experimentation, other colored skins, I'm in,
questions abound
Objectifications, fallacies twisted, like political
jargon
Accepted taboos of aberrant bullshit! (BS)-
unwarranted tests, I flex
Black noise screams from my lips of
Sax ways, jazz ways, ways ahead, dazed...Aged!
Turning musical pages, invoking ancestral sages
Hearing verses of divine speech, vintage
Perfect like Christ's spiritual cipher, non-
decipherable
Sacrificing one discipline, for prophesy sake, my
inner-poise quake
A soul lost to non-spiritual temptation,
One less predestination, sometimes stress in
celestial destination
Revolutionary erotica, the erotic is revolutionary
Tales from the catacombs, underground
Surviving on hollow ground
The dead live on throughout the pages of history
I catch spirits in the wind, like Native Dream
catchers

While souls excavated
Exploited like Hottentots backside
Euro sexual African treasured prizes
Colored pussies suffer from neo-colonial rape
Forced sterilization and experimental surgery,
vilifying!
Xenophobic pirates decimate my pre-existence
Don't be ashamed of the shamed,
For the same shame causes inter-generational pains
Racists' myths perpetuate ignorant energies
Cultivating dilution, convolution, and pollution
Tarnished and tainted, wearing Fanon's mask
Depth of one's essence is lost like "progressive
theory"
And politically incorrect rhetoric
I stand at the juxtapositions of life/death/rebirth
Spiritual intimacy confuses my mind
Like verses from Songs of Solomon
Challenging traditions of sacred psychosexual,
metaphysical
And spiritual inter-connectedness, apprehension is
my life's "raft"
Traditional rituals become caricatures, distortions
of my existence
And now my psyche vacillates as a pendulum
between
Afro-Euro synthesis
An American antithesis
A symbiosis, a mirage of life
Levels of capitalistic conditioning and bargaining
Hope is chronic bliss
Life's corruptions, interruptions

An asili suppressed by Euro odysseys
Like a junkie's hopeless vision of reality
Nigods are vanquished
Straddling cultural identity
Caught up in the plight of others
Sex, love, taboos...
Angelic manifestations rescues my soul
I dance because it is my "Messiah", my liberation
Living between erotic fantasies, lost in a prism of carnal and sacred
Desires to integrate other worlds
Acceptance never achieved, an anomaly always perceived
Experimentations become my soundtrack of lived interludes
Black metaphors keep me dancing in the tenses of time
Diverse women from times past, was it love or a fad? Fading...
Memory of memoirs rarely understood, I understand, over-stood
Encryptions intimacies are scripted on the papyrus of my soul's chest
Passion is lost in a silhouette of kaleidoscopes
Multiple African relationships cultural mixing
Amalgamations (new races/faces) miscegenation once [outlawed]
And hope manifest its complexities in profound moments of anxieties
Provocative lessons in Black and White... strife...we fight!
For an education in necro (death)

Mirroring the reflection of consciousness
/unconsciousness?
Rebirth, a new renaissance in humanity
Cultural pride is exemplified
Sold   Bought
            Packaged
                Repackaged
                    Pressed
    Distributed
            Manufactured
                Marketed
                    Advertised
Managed and
            Produced
We buy! We sell! We buy! We sell! ...
And live the lie of perpetuated hells
Cultural integrity is questioned?
Identity is manipulated through
Cultural theft is confusing, misusing and distorting
our minds
Minds are not sound because race and sex hounds
the flesh
It massages the mind like a 1960's psychedelic drug
Jimi understood the trip, Purple Haze, baby
Music, dance and rhythm cures the curse
Music, dance, and rhythm cures the curse
Music, dance, and rhythm cures the curse
Of Babylon yet the beast lives on
The revolution is erotic, erotic, erotic, erotic...

SOUTH OF ITALY: BRINDISI

We had just arrived in Brindisi, Italy after spending eight hours stuck in a train station up north, in Bologna. Both Justin and I were exhausted from our four-day romp through Firenza (Florence). Our short-lived week took us to Duona, to a museum to view the hype of Michelangelo's *David*, to unknown piazzas, to the shopping district, and to leather flea markets.

We rode mopeds through Tuscany's bright countryside, and skirt-chased enough for a million men. We downed seven seas of Chianti. We could not wait to get down to Corfu, Greece, to explore the twenty-something paradise of the Pink Palace. And after that first night in Corfu, we had stories to add to all of the other surreal ones that we had lived while traveling Europe.

It was about 10:00 A.M. Disillusioned from a sleepless trip, watching out for thieves, and gypsies particularly, we stumbled upon others headed for the Pink Palace.

With all the excitement in the air, we did not realize that, for at least two hours before departing Brindisi, we had to buy tickets and passes *prior* to boarding the boat for Corfu.

While searching for a travel agency, we ran into Tia and Janine, whom we had met in a backpack storage room at the central station in Florence. We had forgotten about them, or at least we told ourselves so. They were as fair as Pacific Island beauties. We approached, and instantly, I decided to ask them to share a room with us in Corfu.

"What's up man?" Tia said. "Anthony, right?"

"Yes, you guessed it. You remember Justin?" I asked.

"Hey! What's up?" Justin chimed, smiling all the while.

"Where are you and your girlfriend headed?" I probed.

"We're going to the Pink Palace!" exclaimed Janine.

"Justin and I will see you there," I said, still not having got around to asking them to share a room.

"Make sure when the boat comes, you save us a spot," Tia insisted.

"Of course, we'll save two beautiful ladies a seat. No problem." I whispered to Justin, "I hope we get to see them in all their splendor." Justin covered his mouth to keep from erupting in impish laughter.

We turned and hurried to buy our tickets and passes for the trip to the Pink Palace. Justin and I were ravenous, and just as fate would have it, we stumbled onto two copper-toned beauties eating what appeared to be an Italian version of a New Orleans style *Poor Boy* sandwich. Though starving like UNICEF children, these women made us momentarily forget our hunger. Lookers always have a way of sidetracking a man's mind.

As far as I was concerned, this was another perfect opportunity to meet more women. Eating could wait. With all the cafés and restaurants around Brindisi, food was an arm's length away.

"How y'all doing?" I asked.

"Fine."

"Where are you ladies from?" I continued.

"We're from New York."

"New York, hunh?"

"Yes."

As I surveyed their bounteousness, I kept saying to myself, "These women are fine as May wine, hot as a July fire cracker, and my loins burn like a December Yule log." It was time to shoot the gift, so I began to shoot.

"How do you call yourselves?" I asked, speaking English in Romance idiom.
"My name is Nadia and this is my cousin Maria. I'm half-Italian, half-Hungarian, and Black by insertion."

Her retort smacked me dead in the face. Did I hear that last part correctly? Nonetheless, I continued.
"How long have you all been in Brindisi, and where're you going next?" I tried to keep a blank face.

"Only a few hours. What about you?" Nadia returned the question.

"We've been here for about six hours now, and we're headed to Corfu," I replied.

I kept thinking about that "black by insertion" comment. Some women will say anything, maybe for the fun of it, maybe just to shock the hell out of you. I thought

Nadia had said that bit for attention. Or maybe she was a bigger freakazoid than either Justin or I imagined.

I looked over at Justin, and his face was registering a strong, but delayed reaction. Bodily he was still composed, but any moment, he would unwind.

"Dude, did you hear her say she that is Black by insertion?" Justin's eyes were as big as pie saucers.

"Yes I did," I whispered to him. "And I'm trying to play it cool and a little slow, but not too slow. Study long, study wrong, and I wanna be right, baby."

Although Justin had known his lion's share of hedonism and roguish adventure, I knew that even he was shocked by Nadia's frankness. Echoing throughout my head was Justin's advice to me on the train ride to Firenza:

"Every moment is an adventure, so take advantage of every moment."

With this in mind, I honed the gift. "Nadia, when the boat gets here, would you and Maria mind sitting with Justin and me?"

"I'd love to keep you company on the boat," she answered with a smile smudged slightly by the sandwich she had been eating.

"Solid!" I said.

A few hours had passed since our early morning peradventure. People were beginning to swarm the port, all with the same destination: the Pink Palace. The sun started to go down, and I began to notice just how beautiful the sea was, even with all the distraction floating around. It was funny looking out, at the Mediterranean, an infinity of azure with a giant peach in it, waiting on a boat to Greece, espying hundreds of young people with oversized and overstuffed backpacks. I felt like an extra in a Hollywood movie about happy-go-lucky Euro-American teens slumming through the Continent, experiencing all of the monumental treasures, all on Daddy's gold card.

Regardless of them, I was glad to be here. In my modern European history classes, I had read about, discussed, debated, and written papers on some of the same historic sites that I had recently found myself in the middle of, touching, sometimes, smelling. I was here to live out as many of my fantasies as possible.

"Anthony the boat's here," Tia alerted me.

"Then, it's time to board the boat, ladies."

"Tia and Janine, you already know Justin. This is Nadia and her cousin Maria."

"Hi," Tia and Janine greeted Nadia and Maria.

"Hello," Nadia and Maria reciprocated.

"Everybody make sure you have all of your suitcases, backpacks, or whatever you're traveling with," I directed.

"Justin, do you have your stuff?" I asked.

"Yeah, Anthony!"

It was a mad house trying to board everybody on the boat. At least three hundred bodies crowded the ramp of the *SS Pink Palace*.

Tia and Janine got lost in the mayhem, just as Nadia, Maria, Justin, and I got on board.

We moved swiftly to secure seats. I made sure that we had space for six reserved. Tia and Janine would have a hard time finding seats. Maria and Nadia got comfortable, and Justin rummaged his pack for snacks.

Eventually, Tia and Janine found us, and took their seats. I began to write in my green leather journal, wielding my silver Cross. Both were going-away presents, given by my colleagues of ten years, who had always encouraged me to write. I noticed Nadia looking over my left shoulder, curiosity pouring out of her eyes, trying to espy my script.

"So, you're a writer?" Nadia asked.

"Yeah. Though, more of a poet."

"Are you going to write a poem for me?"

"If you want. But I don't usually write poetry on demand."

"Would you write something for me, *please*?" She glowed like a ginger, island nymph.

I felt slightly strange about her request. No sooner than I had tried to pen a few verses, Tia and Janine turned around, gawking at me with girlish envy. They did not have to say a word, but they did.

"Anthony, what about *us*. Are you going to write us a poem too?"

"I believe I can dash off something for you," grinning all the
while.

"How long have you been writing poetry, Anthony?" Tia asked.

"For a long time. About fourteen years now.

"Do you plan to write a book soon?" Janine asked.

"Yes, sometime in the very near future. I want to publish my own work."

"Anthony, are you finished with my poem?" Nadia fussed.

"In a minute, dear. I'm almost finished."

> *"An island beauty, tender and sweet.*
> *Timeless like Blue Note jazz.*
> *A lyric freely composed to serenade her*
> *Olive-sheen.*
> *I swim in her ocean, plummeting her treasures,*
> *softly acknowledging the goddess in her."*

"This is for me?" Nadia asked, mildly shocked.

"You did ask for a poem, didn't you?"

"Yes, I did." She leaned over and kissed me on the cheek.

"Are you going to write *us* something, Anthony?" Tia asked again.

"Baby-doll, I'll hook you up when we get to the Pink Palace. Is that alright with you?"

"That's sweet, Anthony. I can't wait."

"Then, it is done."

She Is My Solstice

my tongue holds ancient wisdom
like the wingspan of the Ma'at
42 precepts condensed to the
Ten Commandments
i keep the Metu Neter close to my heart
messages
prophetic
kinetic
Kemetic
cosmic
she is my solstice
her love is lunar, the moon
i am Aten the sun, she's my earth
and i warm her 4x3 hours daily
i give life to her holy landscape
our energy is metaphysical, balanced
my love for her is:
continuous
consistent
constant
celestial
natural
she roams the Universe
illuminating the constellations of Wo'Se Temple
moving from galaxy to galaxy like
gypsies roaming continental surfaces
we are archaic manifestations
in new worlds and old excavated
i am the reincarnation of the wind blowing
atoms scattered throughout time and space

manifesting hue-man-ity desiring the unknown
our love is surreal, ephemeral, seasonal,
misunderstood
1+1=3, I am Ausur, she is Auset we manifest Heru
we chant the wisdom of Tehuti
we stand on the foundation of 5 thousand years
of creation
Stumbling throughout the ages
We live through the pages of the Kemetian Book
of Life
my tongue holds the ancient wisdom of the Ma'at

CORFU

The ride was uncomfortable, not to mention turbulent. The captain thought he would try to make up for lost time by accelerating. The scheduled time of departure from Brindisi had changed several times. From 5:30 to 5:45, from 5:45 to 6:00, from 6:00 to 6:30.

And the trip was overbooked. The boat could not hold half the people who were queued up. The Captain of the *SS Pink Palace* and his crew told us that our travel time would be approximately five and one-half hours. I thought that a bit swift. Eight hours was more like it; but what do I know.

Transportation in Italy is a comedy of errors. The rail and nautical systems have major flaws. Misinformation abounds, and prices for food, souvenirs, not to mention travel itself, fluctuate according to whether it is morning, noon, or night.

Honesty is passé, as it is elsewhere. And *Anglophones* are prey, ready for the picking. The fact that all English or Americans were not rich did not matter. The tourist hunters mistook me for a man of means.

They also mistook me for Ghanaian and for Senegalese, though I speak the king's English very well. But the Italians were clueless. The hue of my skin, my mannerisms, and attire should have alerted them that I did not grow up or live in West Africa. I was no Gold Coast immigrant selling African or Italian kitsch in the piazza.

Eight hours later, across the Mediterranean and Adriatic Seas, we finally arrived on the small island of Corfu. The pitch was so dark that we could not see our hands in front of our faces. All three hundred of us wearily and confusedly disembarked from the *SS Pink Palace.* We walked a slippery slope.

Peering into the night, we heard a convoy of buses rattling and humming in the near distance. Hosts from the tourism agency were supposed to meet and to drive us to the famed Pink Palace hotel. Seasick, we staggered toward the diesel caravan. The drivers took our backpacks and loaded them into the belly of the buses.

Justin, Tia, Janine, and I got on one bus; Nadia and Maria boarded another bus directly behind us. All of us longed for relaxation and sleep. I suspected that my attitude about this trip would brighten with the morning sun.

"Good evening, everybody! I hope your trip over from Brindisi was pleasant. My name is Greg and I'll be your driver." Tia and I looked at each other half-consciously, with a slight grin on our faces, and whispered to each other: "That was a lousy boat ride. He must be kidding."

"I thought the damn thing was going to capsize at the speed it was traveling."

"*You*, I thought I was going to barf on your pants when I turned to you and asked about that poem," Tia reminded me.
"What poem?" I asked.

"The poem you promised me before we boarded the boat."

"Oh, *that* poem."

"Yes, *that* poem," she intoned. "Have you forgotten?"

"Do you have a red dress?"

"*What* . . . what does that have to do with the poem?"
"If you have a red dress, then I already have a title for your poem," I explained.

"As a matter of fact, I do."

"What style?"

"It's a light, strapless evening dress."

"What fabric?" I asked.

"Silk."

"Then, the title's set."

"What is it?"

"*Red Silk in Paradise*."

"I can't wait to read it. Recite a few lines," Tia insisted, a smile insinuating into her mouth.

"No! You'll have to wait," I commanded.

"If that's the way you want it."

"Trust me, Sweet."

The bus ride lasted forever. I kept staring out of the window trying to catch a glimpse of something. But it was darker than pitch's center. As we got closer to the Pink Palace, I noticed the faint glow of lights down in a canyon. We were in outer space; star trekking it, in deep nine, it seemed. Below us, immeasurably deep, was our sybaritic colony. The driver must have been endowed with preternatural powers, for anyone without them would be lost in this space.

The convoy pulled up to the Pink Palace hotel. All ten buses idled in single file. Each bus carried thirty passengers, most of them backpackers who had come over from Brindisi.

The Pink Palace looked like a military compound. As we alighted from the bus and got our backpacks, I noticed how well organized was the staff at the Palace. They retrieved our luggage with soldierly precision, not a movement wasted.

"Anthony, do you see how frickin' huge this place is?" Justin asked.

"Yeah, gargantuan," I said. Let's get inside and see what's happening. Where's Nadia and Maria, though?"

"They're over there, getting their luggage," Justin replied.

"Ladies, I will make sure you get a suite with us," I shouted across the dark distance.

"Okay, we'll see you inside, at the concierge's," Nadia shouted back, exhaustion tinged her voice, but her face was still smiling.

Justin and I walked quickly through the corridor that led to a main entrance that led to a room called the Seaside Registration Office. Again, this was a precise and detailed operation. Everybody in the office was young, white, and seemed to be overly energetic, waiting for the next rush of Palace guests with alacrity.

Justin and I started to arrange our papers for check-in. Unfortunately, we had to stand in a line longer than the Appian Way. After an hour or so, we made it to the counter. The receptionist asked us for identification, a credit card, our passes, and registration forms.

"Good evening, gentlemen. How are you tonight?" asked ALANA the receptionist. She wore a fifties-stripe, white and navy henley with cropped alabaster chinos. Her sun-drenched bob highlighted the freckles on her celestial nose.
"Fine. Thank you. We're just exhausted from the trip," added Justin.

At this point, I didn't really want to talk. All I wanted was to find our room and hit the sack. Alana pulled out a list with names on it, and carefully scanned the list to see if our names were on it, and to make sure we had been assigned a room.

"Ah, yes, here you are. You two are in suite 110—"

"Where's that?" Justin asked, interrupting Alana.

"Well, here's a map. Follow the blue points and it will lead you to your suite."

"How far is it from the beach?" I asked.

"It's a fifteen-minute walk from your suite. As a matter of fact, you're not far from the water," Alana informed us.

"How many beds are in the room, Alana?" I asked.

"There are two bunk beds, which can accommodate four people."

"Then, can we add two of our friends to our room?" Justin queried.

"Yes, since you two are the only ones registered for this suite. I see no problem. But I'll need to know the names of your friends."

"Nadia Patino and Maria Gianni," I stated flatly.

Alana began to scan her list for their names. She flipped through, twice, carefully. Then, she paused and made two crosses through the list.

"I see their names. Where are your friends now?" Alana asked.
I turned my head to see Nadia and Maria walking down the corridor. "Here they come now," I said.

"Ladies, how are you this evening? May I see some identification, your registration and passes, please?"

"Sure, you may," replied Nadia.

After inspecting their papers, in turn, Alana said, "Everything looks fine."

"Thank you," Maria said to Alana.

"Guys, thanks for looking out for us. You saved us a lot of time," Nadia said, smiling, she and Maria juggling their luggage.

Justin and I shouldered our packs, opened up the map, and proceeded out of a backdoor, Maria and Nadia following closely behind. We walked further into darkness. Justin, however, had a flashlight. We looked at the map as we followed a crowd of people going in the same direction as us.

It was around midnight and the temperature was at least 85. The air was thick and sticky. We walked for about ten minutes on uneven gravel, passing a wash room, a swimming pool, a volleyball court, and many suites vaguely resembling Spanish villas.

Finally, we made it to suite 110. We gestured for Nadia and Maria to enter first so as to give them an opportunity to choose where they wanted to sleep. The room was small, approximately twenty feet square, with one window and two bunk beds. It was hotter than Key West in July, and all four of us were bothered.

"Hopefully we can get a better room," Justin appealed to me.

"We will. I'll sign us up for one tomorrow. Something with a nicer view," I encouraged Justin.

"Ladies, are you alright?" I asked Nadia and Maria.
"We'll make it," Maria sighed.

"Damn! I need a smoke. Does anyone smoke?" Nadia asked

"I smoke," Justin piped in. "Here, it's my last one. Do you mind sharing?" Justin asked Nadia.

"Not at all. It's your last square."

"Maria, do you want a drag?" Nadia asked.

"I'm not in a smoking mood right now," insisted Maria.

"Okay, dearest."

After Maria hung a few things in the closet, she left our suite of sweat to see if she could find the beach. She did not ask Justin for his flashlight. She had changed down the hall in the bathroom, and left wearing a tangerine and white, polka-dot bikini. She did not ask Justin for his flashlight. She is very courageous.

Now that we had finally arrived and pitched like bootcampers, all we could do was to try to cool off, and make conversation. I wanted to know what had happened to Tia and Janine. We had not seen them since the bus ride. If I knew Tia, then she would find us before we found her. She was adroit.

I went into the bathroom to change into a pair of clean beige cargo shorts and a white tee shirt. When I came out of the bathroom, Nadia had already slipped into something more comfortable. She wore a pair of white see-through shorts and a gray, ribbed tank top. No panties were visible under her shorts, no bra beneath her top. She had a bush for a *mons* and there was something unusual about her breasts.

"Guys, did you know I have my nipples pierced?" Nadia proclaimed.

"No shit!" Justin and I shouted in surprised unison.

"Do you guys want to see?"

Once again, Nadia had caught me off guard. It was beginning to be a habit. I did not mind it though. Nadia reminded me of

Salomé, full of wily seductions. A part of me thought that she loved attention, and took every moment to bask in it. What were Justin and I supposed to do?

Sitting on the top bunk, in front of us, volunteering to show off her pierced nipples was a sultry, deep olive-toned, part-Italian, part-Hungarian woman. Here was a woman, who in a braggart's tone, had admitted that, in addition to being Italian-Hungarian, she was black by insertion. Perhaps this is why I had decided to come to the Pink Palace in the first place. Perhaps this is why I wanted to spend the first night in the company of Nadia and Maria.

Justin and I tried to ignore Nadia's suggestion. But, again, how were two, flesh-loving men in their mid-twenties to respond? Without any thought, we welcomed her to give us a show.

"Hell yes, we want to see your nipples!"

"Can we take pictures?" Justin asked.

"Get your cameras ready," seduced Nadia.

Justin and I hurried over to our backpacks to get our cameras. Flashes everywhere. An electrical storm. Indra, Zeus, and Thor would be envious.

"Wait! Don't move! Hold that pose! Do that again! Go ahead, girl!" I said.

"Don't stop till I'm out of film," Justin added.

"Girl, do you do this with every stranger you meet?" I asked.

"No, but since it's hot as hell, and I am in Greece, and I'm feeling horny, I thought I would give you guys something to remember me by." Her nipples were naughty, hard, and beaded with perspiration. Her titties were longish as mammoth eggplants.

She climbed off the bunk and waltzed through the room. She gave us full frontal and side views, left and right, right and left. She cupped her titties and pulled on her piercings. She should have been blinded by the flashes, but in this case. She moved closer to me and put her hard-soft nipples on my chest and hugged me tightly. Just as I was about to suck her titties, Maria walked in.

"Nadia, what the hell are you doing, girl? Maria's mouth stood open in shock. I licked my lips.

"Giving the guys a show!" Nadia declared. "Girl don't act like you're all that innocent. I've seen you before," Nadia reminded Maria. "Don't stand there dumbfounded. Come over here and join me!" Nadia teased Maria.

"You big slut! You're such a flirt," reproached Maria.

"Yeah, Maria, do as your cousin says, join her! The camera doesn't bite," Justin assured. I was hoping that Maria had the same prurient streak running through her loins. I had figured that Greece would have many new things to offer. But I had never imagined that which eventually took place in the hot box that first night in Corfu. Even today, I can hardly believe it.

Expecting The Unexpected

I was blown back by the sonic boom of her beauty
I could feel the cadence of her soul beating, moving
slowly
Mirroring the plate tectonic on the ocean floor
I had not cast my eyes upon natural divinity
since the dawn of Christ's ascension
Reveling in her unexpected, was not to be expected
Her sensuality blended like nature's arc in fluidity
of freedom
We indulged the moment, inhibitions free of
constraints
I thought the unthinkable and she revealed the
unbelievable
Episodic moments are to be experienced in the
moment.

10 Biggest Lies At The Pink Palace

1. I'm only staying one night.
2. I know how to ride a moped
3. I'm never drinking ouzo again
4. I'm getting up early tomorrow.
5. Someone else is in my bed; can I sleep with you tonight?
6. I have a boyfriend/girlfriend back home.
7. What, do you think I do this with every girl/guy? (you're special to me)
8. I just want to kiss you...you can keep your clothes on.
9. Of course, I remember your name.
10. No, really. I'm leaving tomorrow.

THE MEDITERRANEAN: IN TOO DEEP

The U.S. and Canadian coterie had just ended a wondrous day zipping around the island of Corfu on mopeds. The weather, as usual, was celestial, reminiscent of Eden. If Adam were here, he would marvel at such a sublime clime.

We had explored every corner of the island, the beaches and the underwater caves. We bathed in clay and dove off hundred-foot cliffs into the sparkling blue of the Mediterranean. We raced our mopeds on desolate, mountain roads. We met gracious, elder Greeks and bought bottles of homemade wine. They had never seen the likes of a Filipino, two Chinese Canadians, one Canadian Indian, along with Justin, Tom, and Mike (white Americans), not to mention myself (a black American). The day had been exciting, yet exhausting, and our crew had cherished every moment of it.

Before we knew it, the day was coming to an end, and we began the trek back to the Pink Palace. Dinner would be served on time, as always. Scheduled events, like meals, unfolded with military precision at the Pink Palace.

Hot and sticky, hungry and dehydrated, irritable and tired, we returned from our sunny peradventures. Earlier in the day, it would seem that Cupid or Priapus had been spotted once or twice. Now, I wondered what the evening would bring.

The only women in the group were Tia and Janine. Both of them were fantastically sculpted goddesses who dripped sensuality from every pore. Needless to say, the men in our group were smitten, bitten by the *Lustprinzip*. They wanted a taste of so-called Eastern exoticism. The sexual tension spread like Frisco fog. Corfu had a way of inflaming the libido.

I focused on how to approach Tia. None of the guys realized that I had already shot the gift to Tia, back in Brindisi. Tia, Janine, and I had sat together on the boat ride to Corfu. On the second day of our visit, the three of us rented mopeds and rode to a secluded swimming hole, where we lunched, talked, and of course, swam. On the boat to Corfu, Tia and Janine had been enthralled by my poetry and begged me to write poems for them. I had not yet gotten around to composing anything, but saw it as a perfect opportunity to slip in a subliminal line or two.

While everyone else wanted to return to their bungalows to rest and to change for dinner, I, on the other hand, wanted to make a few journal entries about Corfu. I had promised myself to capture all on paper.

After returning my moped, I decided against going to my bungalow. Instead, I went to the bathroom, washed, and headed to the dining area. The queue was already long, but I soon got my dinner, joined the clique at table, and ordered drinks. A slight breeze blew, and I comfortably awaited the nighttide. But before I could get lost in thoughts of what was to come, Nadia and Maria appeared out of nowhere. Their beauty shone like a newborn sun blessing the rosy dawn. And their presence sparked competition amongst the gentler sex.

"Anthony, who are your *friends*?" Nadia asked cattily.

"This is my Canada-California connect. I would love to introduce everyone, but all of you can speak for yourselves," I replied. Then, I got up to leave, and Nadia said, "Just where do you think you're going?"

"To freshen up! I'll be back in an hour. I'll meet you all at the Palladium. I need to get my groove on, badly. Tension's got me tight," I explained.

"Can I help you unleash some tension tonight," Nadia teased.

"You got jokes, girl," I remarked, smiling all the while.

The crew looked snidely at Nadia.

"She had to sneak another one in, huh?" Justin whispered in my ear.

Tia and Janine glanced at Nadia and Maria, as if to say, "These bitches just stole our fire!" But Nadia and Maria were a blessing in disguise because their presence would give me leverage with Tia and Janine.

On the way to my bungalow, I stopped at one of the outdoor bars, and quaffed two Grolsch. Sitting there, I marveled over the situation: two pairs of ravishing lookers vying with each other to be the center of the male gaze. Tia and Janine were Asian, from Toronto, while Nadia and Maria were Italian-Americans from the eastern seaboard. All I could do was laugh into my beer and recall David's words, when we were in Barcelona: "Every moment should be an adventure." Judging by the catty encounter between Nadia and Maria and Tia and Janine, the night might venture past adventure.

My bungalow was a two-room, Spanish-style villa, nestled in a cove of the beach, protected by a narrow walkway, camouflaged by a verdant canopy of luxuriant plants and palm trees that lounged obliquely beneath a veil of azure. The stroll to the sea took less than five minutes. Though more picturesque than the hot box shared by Nadia, Maria, Justin, and I, on the night of our arrival, my bungalow lacked that certain claustrophobic intensity and rawness of the hot box. But here was paradise.

While showering, I could faintly hear water rippling the shore. Echoes of festive conversation burst in harmonious chords. I was amazed to hear anything at all, over the soft cacophony of showers splashing me. My ears became tympanums of euphoria. Heaven and earth merged, and I was caught betwixt, in a deluge of bliss.

I dried off, brushed my teeth, rubbed cocoa butter on my body and lined my scalp with hemp. I donned a fresh pair of boxers, denim knickers, a white linen shirt, and sandals. Before leaving the bungalow, I fisted a pocketful of drachmas, choked a Grolsch, found the mini-flashlight, and headed to the disco.

Outside was darker than the center of pitch. You could not see a white ghost in front of you. The line at the Palladium was longer than one at a Skid Row liquor store on the first of the month. I maneuvered my way to the front. There, I saw a Ugandan sister from England. I had first seen her in Brindisi, about the same time that I met Nadia and Janine. Maya was her name and she was adorable enough, but apparently she was not checking for a brother. She seemed aloof and arrogant, yet I struck up a conversation anyway. Besides, I wanted to use her as an excuse to cut the queue.

"Maya, what's up girl? Are you still holding my place in line?" I yelled.

"What? Are you serious?"

"As serious as stale chittlins. Here I come. Hold on."

I crossed to the very front of the queue and began shooting the gift. Maya was a little astonished, to say the least. She had this look in her eyes, as if to say, "You got some nerve." But I did not care what the *fuck* she thought. She owed me this, since she had snubbed me on our first encounter. What better way to get reacquainted?

"Thanks for waiting. You look ravishing this evening," I smirked.

"You have got some nerve, not to mention that you're hasty."

"Work with me, girl. All this will be over in a moment. I'll buy you a drink when we get inside. Just follow the flow.

"Okay. But you owe me, major!"

"I got this. Don't fret the moment; find the adventure in it."
We entered the Palladium at the Pink Palace, a distorted image of a fictional couple. It worked nonetheless.

Immediately, I scanned the crowd for diamonds. There were a lot of sapphires and jasmines. Maya followed on my heel, profiting from the swath that I cut through the thicket of bodies. Maya was a paragon of loveliness. She was slimmer than Naomi Campbell, and butterscotch of hue. Long, midnight tresses framed a set of hazel eyes that pierced granite. Sidling up to the bar, we waited for service.

"Bartender, I would like to buy the lady a drink."

"I'll be with you in a moment, let me help these people over here first," said the bartender.

"So, Maya, ready to drink?" I asked.

"Yes!"

"What shall it be?"

"I'm feeling like sex on the beach."

"Really!"

"Yes."

"Why not a screwdriver in the wall?"

"I beg your pardon . . . What did you say?"

"I said, 'Why not a screwdriver against the wall?'"

"Are you being fresh with me?"

"No. Look, Maya . . . thanks for helping out in line. I just wanted to repay the favor, even if you didn't mean it."

Maya looked at me with a very wry smile. I tried to pay it as little attention as possible. I simply wanted to have one drink with her and to return to the coterie, but the bartender was nowhere to be found. I had hoped to spot Nadia and Maria or Tia and Janine, but they were conspicuously absent.

Eventually the bartender reappeared. He was a half-pink fellow with a gregarious smile. His swiftness and cheer amazed me; he seemed indefatigable, unfazed.

"What is the lady drinking this evening?" the bartender asked.

"A Sex on the Beach," I said.

"This is my first time, you know?"

"How do you mean?" I asked.

"I've never had Sex on the Beach before," Maya revealed. I hope I like it."

"And what are you having, sir?" the barman inquired.

"I welcome sex on the beach, but I'm a barley man. How about a Guinness Stout?"

"One Sex on the Beach and one Guinness coming up!"

Waiting for our drinks, I squinted through clouds of smoke and blinding strobes to discover the clique at an oblong table against the far wall. All appeared all right. Next to me, Maya's lips pouted and her eyes flitted about, avoiding mine. The bartender finally brought our drinks, and I availed of the opportunity to quit Maya. Evidently, she was not interested.

Tia, Janine, Nadia, and Maria looked catty, seductive, primed, and without peer. They had a don't-talk-to-me-if-you-don't-know-me aura about them. I was glad to know them for I had decided to talk to one of them, but I did not know which one. Approaching the table I started in.

"What's up y'all?"

"Nothing! Just chilling, drinking, and listening to the music," Tia replied.

"Anthony, what's up with *you*?" Nadia followed.

"I'm excited about getting on the dance floor and moving like the Nicholas Brothers."

"Moving like whom? Who are the Nicholas Brothers?" Maria asked

"They're famous African-Americans who set the standard for elegance and stylish intricate movement back in the 30s-50s for tap-dancers. They were quintessence African artistry in motion."

"A metaphor for a good dancer," Maria put in.

"Yes, precisely! You got it. Does anyone what to *Nicholas*?" I asked.

Everyone seemed too tired, too tipsy, too bored, or too antipathetic to the scene. I did not want to believe that any cohort chose not to dance because she or he felt incapable. Everybody knows how to dance. Regardless of the figures, dancing is simply movement.

I wanted to ask both Nadia and Tia to dance simultaneously, but decided upon a less obvious course. I asked everyone at the table to dance, and they reluctantly agreed. Like a lark, I flew to the floor, glad to see my mates getting off of their asses. No one should have felt pressure, expectation, or consequence from such simple gesture.

Group dancing can assume strange-looking forms. An octopus with eight heads might appear. It might do the lindy hop or jitterbug, the Charleston or the wop, the robot or the Virginia reel, the smurf or the butterfly, the Mobile buck or the electric boogaloo all at one time. Personally, I never attempted to mimic any figures, to follow any standard strut. Simply, I did my thing. On this particular night, pulling Nadia was my thing.

We began freaking at once. Body-kinetic-electric shocked us together. She grabbed me; I grabbed her. My hands roamed sacred places, and her face whispered silent liturgies. She pressed her ass up against my Priapus, and I dug a hole to China via Mars.

We coupled with purple dance, music, sex, and romance. Everyone else had perished in 1999, but we had escaped in a red Corvette. We were afflicted with night fever, and the doves cried for us. When the roof caught fire, we came to and realized that the all of the crew screwed us, their mouths agape, not knowing whether to smile, frown, or feel embarrassed, if not for ourselves, then for their own selves. Instead, they cheered.

"Go Anthony . . . Go Nadia . . . Freak him, girl! Show him the dime and the dinkum," Maria yelled.

Of course, by this time, the guys were pumping me. A circle of revelers surrounded us. They mimicked our dance. So enraptured was I that I had failed to notice Tia's departure. Where had she gone?

Scanning the floor for her, my periphery caught two girls staring at me. I thought that they wanted to eat me, so I, too, left the circle. Before accosting them, I prepared the gift. I did not want anyone to beat me to that proverbial punch.

"Hey! What's up? Come over and shimmy with me, ladies," I stated baldly.

"Sure," they cordially replied.

"Where're you girls from?"

"We are from Switzerland! I am Gerry, and this is Danielle."

"Where are *you* from?" Danielle asked.

"I'm from California."

"Where in California?" asked Gerry.

"The Bay Area. San Francisco via Oakland."

"Great! How do you like Greece?" inquired Danielle.

"Right, now, it feels like paradise. I love it!"

"We are glad that you are having fun. Are those your friends over there?" Gerry probed.

"Yes, they are," I said.

"Is *that* girl your girlfriend?" Danielle asked boldly.

"Those are my friends, but she, Nadia, is *not* my girlfriend."

Before Danielle could follow with another question—her lips were parted as if to speak—someone tapped me on the shoulder. I turned around to behold Tia holding a creamy, brown drink in a snifter. 'Twas strange. What the hell was it? The beer had already loosened a few sheets, and I had adopted an old adage about mixing drinks: "Liquor after beer, if you drink liquor; if you don't drink liquor, then stick to beer."

"This is for you!" and Tia extended her arm. "I thought you could use some refreshment after that last performance."

"Thanks for being so concerned. Appresheate your kindness, Tia," I slurred. "By the way, this is Danielle and this is Gerry. They are from Switzerland. That makes them Swiss Misses. Gerry and

Danielle, this is Tia. She's from Canada," I finished the round of introductions.

"Hi," the Swiss greeted Tia.

"Hello," Tia replied.

"Are you going to dance with me, Tia?" I expectantly asked— I expected her to say yes.

"No, thank you. I'm content to watch."

"Come on girl, dance with daddy!" I prodded.

"I'll see you in a moment, Anthony," and she calmly stepped away.

"You sure you don't want to dance?" I called after her. She came back and whispered in my ear, "We'll dance later . . . my way."

Turning to the Swiss Misses, I saw them both eyeing me, succubi fingering their grins. "Wanna dance?" I asked them.

"Of course," they brightened.

We bumped the grind and freaked foreplay. Danielle and Gerry were so enthusiastic, much easier than Sunday morning.

Less than fifteen minutes later, I feel another tap on my shoulder, from the front this time. But I cannot see who it is because my eyes are glued shut. "Anthony . . . Anthony . . . Anthony . . . Anthony . . . Anthony . . . Anthony . . . Anthony!" a voice was calling me, each time crescendo.

Tia extended her arm again, and it held another creamy, brown drink. "What am I drinking, darling?" I finally inquired.

"Bailey's. That's two in a row. I see that you liked it."

"Yeah—"

"Then drink and be merry, for you can't drink in hell," and Tia laughed very mischievously.

What was she thinking? And how long would she keep this up? I took the drink, as I did the last, in good faith, and continued my Swiss sandwich.

"You are an awesome dancer," Danielle yelled over the music, her mouth a perfect O.

"Yeah, Anthony, you are a sexy-terrific dancer. I love the way you move," Gerry added, all the while caressing her tresses.

"You ladies don't move too badly yourselves." I kept wondering where this ball was headed.

Before I could slide into good rotation, I felt another tap on my shoulder. I looked behind me this time, and there was Tia with yet another Bailey's. Inasmuch as I was still holding a more than half-full snifter, Danielle and Gerry, for the first time, began to stare very curiously at Tia, and at me.

The drink already in my hand—I downed it, a single gulp. When I reached for the third drink, my stomach almost peeled in my mouth, my knees buckled, and a hot typhoon swept my body. I momentarily recovered and decided to get to the point.

"Woman, what do you want with me? Why do you keep bringing me all of these mutherfucking drinks?"

"I . . . I . . . I . . . don't know what I want," she admitted.

"You must want *something.* You keep bringing me all these drinks!"

"I . . . I want to . . ."

Before she could respond, I—somewhat out of kilter—grabbed both of her hands, and pulled her to my chest. We began kissing as lost lovers who thought they would never kiss again. Tightly we held each other, and I rested my hand in the small of her back. I thought she would pull back, and turn away, but she stayed.

Standing there amidst a tumult of strange bodies, I pressed my lips to hers. Eyes bore a hole through both of us. When I opened my own eyes, shock washed the faces of Danielle, Gerry, Justin, Tom, Mike, Nadia, Maria, and Janine. With our lips still locked, I looked at Tia, and she looked as if she had not been kissed in twenty years.

"Tia, where are you? Are you here with me?" I asked.

"Yes! I'm here . . . I'm . . . here, Anthony. How are you?"

"Fifty sheets to the wind, but grand! I'm a bit light-headed, but not from the Bailey's," I laughed.

"So what now?" she asked.

"You tell me."

"I want to go skinny-dipping in the sea," she uttered, nervously.

"You want to do what, where? Did you say you want to *skinny-dip* right now?"

"Yes! Let's go; it'll be fun. We can invite the crew!"

"You're joking, right? It's darker than a night of ravens out there."

"Anthony, I'm feeling adventurous. I need to cool off. Besides, you're the one always talking about taking the ride, about welcoming all adventures."

"Girl, I can barely walk. I might drown."

"Just trust me. We'll all go together. Everything will be fine. I promise."

Tia had presented me with a dilemma. On the one hand, her idea was awesome—how many times in life does one skinny-dip in the Mediterranean, at night, with a beautiful woman? On the other hand, what black man in his right mind would take his ass out into unknown waters, at night, where who-knows-what type of shit might be lurking? Of course, Tia would be standing there in all her bounty and splendor. The thought of it had me open like a passage to India.

But I could not fathom being in the sea at night, naked with the coterie. Though it would be pitch-black, and none of us would see a damn thing. I glanced at Tia, then at Janine, and thought, why not. Tia wore a peculiar expression. I interpreted it as having something to do with her beau back in Toronto. She had mentioned him more than once. Ironically, he was from Greece—Patras, I believe.

Our second day in Corfu—those ambrosial hours of swimming holes and mopeds—Tia and I had related our travels to each other. She had asked me how many flings I had had. Obligingly, I told her only one. We talked some more, but I refrained from asking about her affairs, I wanted the mystery her essence to present. Instead we drank wine and chased it with shots of ouzo. Then, when the wine flew us through the wind and the ouzo oozed out of our pores, Tia tried to push me off on her cousin Janine, but not before telling me of her beau from Patras. Still, I was not into Janine; I found Tia much more intriguing.

Eventually, we left the Palladium. I bid goodnight to the Swiss Misses, as Tia and I headed for the exit. We evanesced into Ionian darkness. Our ten-minute walk stretched eternally, as we staggered down blind trails leading to the sea. Tia draped me like an over-sized cloak. Above the moon hung low, silhouetting us in the majesty of dusk. Rocks scraped our feet, while cool sand soothed us.

We tossed our clothes aside a few feet from the tide. Hand in hand, we dashed to into the waters. Tia jumped on my back, wrapping her legs around my waist. The warmth of her body and the soft, moistness of her vagina kissed my loins. I seesawed on the precipice of desire.

Grabbing Tia by her thighs, I pulled her in front of me. We kissed, drank from each other's mouth, moaning from the thirst of anticipation. Tia stared into my eyes as if peering into an aperture of the stars.

"Anthony, what are you feeling?"

"I'm feeling heaven right now. You're divinity."

"Do you want me? Do you want this? Tell me what you need," she pleaded.

"Yes. Yes. You, I want and need this moment." I replied.

"Do you really want me?"

"Yes. From the moment I saw you in Florence at the train station, and when you asked me to write an "ode" for you on the boat ride over."

"I just wanted you to think about me. Then, the day that you, Janine, and I spent together confused me."

"Why?"

"Because I kept thinking about my boyfriend back home, but my body was thinking of you."

"So, what now?"

The night was calm. The moon shone alone without a star in sight. I could feel the plate tectonic beneath our feet. We gracefully tread water like two aquatic amphibians. Tia's body relaxed into my hands like soft silk caressing my skin.

"I want to feel your words inside of me. Write a poem here,"
and Tia reached down and slowly touched her mons. "Move me like
the ripples of the sea."

Chance

A chance encounter serenaded by island ambiance
A tropical paragon, beauty mysterious, refine,
celestial, beloved
You are an anachronism familiar from time past,
blessing my presence
Dare I express my thoughts to you in 1000
ways?
Do I silence my tongue,
to allow imagination to indulge infinite possibilities?
Your eyes are cryptic visions of the unknown,
Secrets lying deep within a fortress of desires,
waiting.
Metal orgasms concede your spirit 1000 times
before touched
May I be tactile, freely painting lyrically
on the canvas of your mind?
Allowing for indelible artistic impressions and
expressions
Words are worth more than material possession,
They are treasures caressing, contours of your
essence
Chance is all we have, sometimes seen/unseen.
Be. Become. Beguile me with your synergy, your
energy.
May my words soothe your mind like the hand of
Jah,
massaging your spirit
You are a chance encounter serenaded by
island ambiance.

CHIVALRY IN CORFU:
EPILOGUE FOR A SISTAH

Maya in Hindu is a symbol of temptation. Moreover, she is a courtesan. I first learned of Maya while reading the *Kama Sutra*. According to Vedantic philosophy, Maya is a representation of the illusion of sensory experience and of the experienced qualities and attributes of oneself. Maya is neither good nor evil.

One early morn before Aurora had spread her fingers of rose, I found myself in a most unexpected situation. For the past eight hours, I had been at the Palladium, immersed in a strobe light microcosm of Brave New World ecstasy. I emerged with blurred vision and noodles for legs. My sole wish was to sleep until the millennium.

Salt filled the air and heat stuck to every pore. A slight Afer wind kissed my face and a tropical slumber overcame me. Darkness still donned its cloak and Venus had not yet abdicated her eastern throne. But a strange voice, choked with struggle and fear, interrupted my reverie. I listened cautiously to discover from whence it came.

As I followed my ears, my eyes promptly beheld a man slight of frame. He was poking and probing, flagrantly groping a woman, whom I could not clearly see. I could hear her though—she had a British accent. Behind her stood another fellow, nonchalantly observing the scene. Walking closer, I saw frenzy twisting the woman's face.

"Get your bloody paws off me, you obnoxious prick!" she screamed.

"Don't play hard to get. I like pretty black girls. You come to Corfu for pleasure, yes," taunted Italian machismo.

"I told you already, I'm not interested. Please leave me alone, you bloody bastard."

But this Italian simply did not understand the word, "No!" And the man of Nordic visage showed no sign of intervening. Instead, a wily grin snaked across his lips. It was at this point that I decided to jump in. However, before I could take a further step, the Italian rifled the woman's blouse and began to squeeze her ass. She screamed so hard that it curdled the salt air. I rushed without thinking. I clutched the man by his neck and flung him a few feet back. He stumbled before catching the toe of his shoe on his other heel, and fell.

"What the hell is wrong with you?" I roared, standing astride the Italian. "The lady doesn't want to be bothered. Can you understand that?"

The woman looked at me with relief and surprise. She must not have seen me approach. I wondered what had happened. Were they together? Was the Italian some Jack the Ripper type? And who was the Scandinavian still standing nonchalantly?

As I turned to see if the woman was alright, the Italian quickly got to his feet and pulled on my arm. I spun to him, and he stepped close to my face, a nose-length away. I stared straight at him with 400 years of rage and balled my fists. He raised his right hand as if to cross me. I stepped back, hooking a left to his jaw. He stumbled, tripped, and fell again. I ran to him and launched my thirteen's into his rib cage. He yelled like a milksop and I kicked him again. He rolled on his side, grabbing himself as if he had lost something valuable. I spit on him and hurried to the woman. She was sitting on the ground, pulling her knees to her chest, gently rocking back and forth. The Scandinavian was nowhere in sight. I quickly glanced back to the Italian. He was hugging himself, still as a lullaby.

"Are you okay?" I inquired.

"Yes. Thanks so much. Your timing could not have been better. You came like the redcoats."

"I'm not a redcoat nor a Yankee, and definitely not a Confederate. I just don't like to see a woman in distress."

"Thank you."

"Are you sure you're alright?" I asked again.

"Yes. I am secure."

"Do you need anything?"

"Just . . . walk with me," she said, her arms tightly wrapped around her bosom.

"Where to?"

"Home!"

"Where is home?"

"A six-minute walk from here."

"Good. Then we shall head for refuge and sanctity. "

"That would be stupendous. You are truly an angel."

"Not an angel, just a Black Knight, maneuvering through the night protecting you from the beguiling elements of a precarious episode."

"You are truly my Messiah right now."
"I am not Jesus, but I'll accept the complement as 'Savior' tonight! There are good people left on earth. It's just unfortunate humanity doesn't willingly extend it hand to those in need."

"Right...I think there's much to be said about genuine kindness. You make a good case. Was I your case study, this morning?"

"No, I was acting out of fear, concern, and compassion. Last I checked, those attributes don't rank to high on the totem pole of life. Most people are afraid to help others in need, and rarely get involved to potential stop a situation that could result into dire consequence. I am sure you would have done the same for me, if circumstance was similar."

"Yes...I would have assisted, you. How I don't know, but I would have tried to help better your situation, if it appeared to rather capricious ordeal. Yes, definitely."

"That is good to know."

As Aurora spread her fingers and Ra charged his barque, we walked along the beach, before finally settling on the warm sand. She was younger than I had thought; apparently fear had temporarily aged her. I learned that she hailed from England.

Though she was black like me, her language, mores, aesthetics, tastes for food, clothes, life, and men were thoroughly British. I learned that she was actually afraid of black men, so she never talked to or dated them. These insights of this woman may have been true after having untimely discourse and discovering her true nature. I believed by the end of this ordeal, and given time to reflect on what transpired for her this morning, she will have come to recognize the beauty in her own men and quite possibly have a different revelation of the wellspring from whence she came.

Her name was Maya.

Combination Skin

Two nations, East African and British
In passing, we met, our eyes locked,
We kept walking
Her silence spoke volumes without an utterance of
a word
She left a subtle scent summoning me, discreetly
I was drawn to her as a moth to a flame
Skin, a chestnut colored hue,
Ashanti almond-shaped eyes
Hair wooly like lamb's skin, midnight black, soft
A walk graceful embodying heaven's arc
She inspired a new conversation seducing me with
age-old decadence
I sensed she had an objection to my person, yet
curiosity abounded
Her upbringing prohibited her from connecting
with my soul
Two worlds, two polar opposites, two continents,
two kinds of Africans
Maybe the difference is what we had in common
Combination of skins, of cultures, of languages, of
worldviews,
We were connected, more than either of us were
willing to admit
She became a metaphor for the soundtrack of
my world, instantaneously
Every beauty I met was of combination skin

SWISS MISSES: A TRAIN RIDE

The Pink Palace is another chapter in Black History, another tale of an expatriate-to-be.

I am en route to Paris. Still echoing in my mind are the words of Duke and Richard (two guys I met in Corfu): "Never pass up bliss. Shut the hell up, and drink!" Duke and Richard knew how to party, and they lived every moment *in* the moment. The fact that they were moneyed and did not have a care in the world facilitated their wassailing, merry-making, smoking, and fornication with every woman with a tight, curvaceous derrière—and even those without one.

Two and a half months have passed, and I miss home. Corfu is behind me, and the Ionian and Adriatic Seas ahead. Loneliness settles in, as does that nervous void in my stomach, like unto when a girlfriend cheats or a lover leaves. For the past two weeks, Corfu has been my mistress, more than a one-night stand, more like steps to celestial ascension.

This morning, I left the Pink Palace with a caravan of bohemians, whoremongers, adulteresses, liars, cheaters, spoiled brats, trust-fund babies, vagabonds, intellectuals, right-wing conservatives, left-wing radicals, confused liberals, freaks, lascivious Italians in spandex with egos larger than St. Peter's Cathedral, and coconuts. Coconut is a term that refers to blacks in England who prefer to celebrate their European acculturation and to suppress their African heritage. Stateside, we call the latter Oreos. Looking at all these people and labeling them was sadistic humor; and satirical poetry.

The journey back to northwestern Europe would take two days by rail. I longed for France because I wanted to decompress and to reflect on my travels in the comfort of Aunt Rachel's flat in Neuilly. I also fancied making junkets to Luxembourg and Austria via Paris. And perhaps, there was something new in store for me there.

I purchased my ticket for the ferry departing for Brindisi (Italy). This leg of the trip would take six hours. I did not mind the return voyage, since I would be traveling by ferry as opposed to the large speedboat, as on the way over.

At 8:00 A.M. the ferry arrived at the Port of Corfu. The majority of the passengers were Italians returning home. Also, many callow, but vibrant Americans were traveling. Besides me, I noticed only one other black. I surmised that he was Nigerian. Yet, after the episode with Maya, I did not take his sable complexion as a sign that we had anything in common.

When the time came to board the ferry, the agent checking passports and tickets asked me, "From where do you hail?" At the time, I did not think anything of her question. However, the question unsettled me inasmuch as none of the passengers immediately in front of me were asked from whence they came.

Once aboard, I made way to the outer part of the ferry in order to find a place to rest and to protect myself from the thieves aboard. Eventually, I found a small alcove of sorts. I was utterly exhausted and my subconscious badgered me to stay awake. Words from the Koran echoed in my head: "Trust Allah, but tie your camel." Heeding these words, I hid some of my monies and my passport under my outer garment. The other monies and credit cards I secured in my briefs. Then, I fell asleep.

Despite what the agents insisted, the ride from Corfu would take at least eight hours. When I awoke, I checked my watch to discover that the trip was half over. My valuables were intact, and I felt somewhat rejuvenated. Desiring to chat with a few Americans, I walked portside. There, I ran into a group of Californians. We casually conversed until I got bored, and I returned to my alcove.

About four hours later, the ferry pulled into Brindisi, in southern Italy. Things had come full circle: I returned to where I had first met Nadia and Maria. A sudden uneasiness spread through me, followed by a mad rush of passengers for the exit. People pushed, stumbled, fell down, and climbed over one another. I stood back and watched, glad that I had dodged the Technicolor yawn of maritime.

On the gangplank, I noticed the other agent who had checked passports and tickets upon boarding for Brindisi. He was sniffing like a hound dog. When my turn came, he studied my passport and other identification. Then, Alfonzo, the ticket agent, pulled me aside and searched my pack and passport (again).

"May I see your passport?" Alfonzo asked.

"Of course, you may," I replied.

After much scrutiny, he looked at me nonplussed. That same nervous feeling flooded me. Alfonzo tightened his grip on the little blue book.
"Are you African?"

"Yes. I'm African American," I declared.

"I didn't ask if you are an African American. Are you an African?"

"No! Actually, I'm American."

Still dumbfounded, Alfonzo asked me to follow him. He led me to a detainment room inside the ferry. There he battered me with one question after another, casting supreme doubt on my existence. It crossed my mind that my passport might be seized. Possibly, I might be stuck in Italy, detained indefinitely at immigration headquarters. I hoped that the American Embassy was nearby. Their questions were redundant, to say the least.

"Your name is Anthony?" Alfonzo asked.

"Yes, as it appears on my passport!" I added sarcastically.

"Do you have any other forms of identification proving your nationality?"

"Are you serious, sir? You need proof other than a valid passport to prove my nationality?"

"Yes! I do."

"Do you detain everyone like this?"

"Excuse me. What did you say?"

"Why such flagrant harassment? What more do you need from me?"

"We require other forms of photo identification. A passport simply isn't good enough."

Digging into my backpack, I pulled out my college ID, my driver's license, my California State ID, my old international student ID, my hostel ID, a YMCA membership card, and my Berkeley

Public Library card. Needless to say, I was hotter than Mercury.
The search yielded nothing, and I was finally let go. I could not wait
to leave Brindisi. Paris promised peaceful refuge. I found myself
wanting to rattle of many unkind expletives at Alfonzo, but my
spiritual voice directed me to do otherwise, lest I wanted to stir up
any more harassment from Gambino's cousins. After all southern
Italians did not take too kindly to the African cousins. It seemed to
be a history of denial for many of them; disrespecting the blueprint
of ancient history.

Upon arrival at the station, I thumbed through my timetable. I
found a train departing Brindisi, headed for Paris via Milan and
Switzerland. The trip would still take approximately two days. Not
looking forward to the long ride, thoughts of first class consoled me.
I desired serenity, but questions of my identity pricked me. What did
it mean to be a black American in Europe? Apparently, the Italians
pegged me for African: Ethiopian, Ghanaian, Nigerian, anything
except American. My reality and sense of self were being
challenged to the core. None of my experiences in America could
help me here.

Finding an empty bench, I doffed my pack and stretched out to
rest. The train would not leave for several hours. As I closed my
eyes, familiar voices called from across the station, behind me. I
hesitated to turn around because I did not feel like talking to anyone.
Suspicion mixed with curiosity started to gnaw away at me, so I
turned around. There were Gerry and Danielle, the Swiss Misses
from the Palladium in Corfu.

"Anthony is that you?" Gerry asked.

"What's up ladies? What a wonderful surprise!"

"Where are you going next?" Danielle asked.

"I'm off to Paris to reconnect with my family. Where are you
lovelies going?"

"We are headed back to Switzerland. Gerry is going to Lausanne and I am going to Zurich."

"Sounds great. We're going to be on the same train for a day or so," I explained.

"Yes, we will. We look forward to traveling with you," Gerry said.

"Anthony, have you paid for your supplements yet?" Danielle asked.

"No, I've been procrastinating. I don't really want to pay any more fees."

"Then don't worry about it. Let us take care of the fees for you," Gerry generously offered.

"I can't let you do that. I can handle the fees myself."

"We insist. You are a guest in our part of the world. Relax and enjoy your trip to France. There is no problem," Gerry assured.

"Yeah, don't worry, handsome. We will do you the honor," Danielle smiled.

"Well, if you insist . . . I can't stop your altruism."

"Then it is done. Once we pay, let us get some food for the train," Gerry added.

"Okay, but let me take care of the food. It's the least I can do."

"No, we are purchasing the food too. All you have to do is relax and enjoy the trip," Gerry persisted.

"So, is there a catch to all of this? What's with all this generosity?" I asked, suspicion tingeing my voice.

"We just want you to relax and have fun. You seemed a little full of angst," Danielle explained.

"What gave you that impression?"

"We saw you being detained on the ferry, and frankly, the situation did not look too pleasant. We were wondering what was happening. If you were alright," Gerry said.

"No. I'm a bit shaken, but it'll pass."

"We thought that perhaps we could make your travel easier," Danielle said, apparently sincere.

"Thanks. I didn't know anyone was paying attention."

Admittedly, I was very suspicious. Did Gerry and Danielle have some sort of hidden agenda? I couldn't figure it. Never in the States had I known such kindness. I recalled what an African in a Paris café had related to me once over dinner. This man had known many women from all over the world. "If you want to be financially secure, my friend, you should marry a Swiss woman," he said. "Swiss women are intelligent, generous, and extremely good with money. It's in their nature."

In retrospect, he seemed to have a point. Here I was with two Swiss women whom I barely knew, and they were paying for my supplements and dinner. Still, I wondered if they harbored ulterior motives. Maybe Gerry and Danielle had never met a black man from the States, and Negrophilia had infected them.

Four hours later, the three of us boarded the train without incident. We quickly found our first-class cabin and settled in. The air was calm and inhibitions non-existent. I took advantage of the situation to find out more about Gerry and Danielle.

"So where are you two from?"

"I am from Lausanne, Switzerland," Gerry stated playfully.

"And I am English, but living and teaching in Switzerland, Danielle responded woodenly.

"Have either of you been to the States?"

"Yes. I actually study at Vanderbilt University," Gerry replied.

"Really! How do you like the South?"

"It's great! There are lots of cool people there. Your history is intriguing to say the say the least. People there treat me differently because I am from Europe," Gerry insisted.

"What do you mean when you say people treat you differently?"

"Well, the blacks there don't treat me like a Southern white woman. They don't see me as an enemy, and are usually friendly to me. The white people don't understand how we get along so well. But the blacks, I mean the African Americans, are warm and receptive, so easy to get along with, if you are open."

"So you have many black friends back in the States?"

"Yes. I am returning there this fall to finish my studies."

"What are you studying?"

"I am studying law and politics," Gerry informed me.

"Why come to the States to study law and politics? Why not go to Oxford, Cambridge, the Sorbonne?"

"I wanted to get a different perspective. I have visited New York, Los Angeles, San Francisco, but never had I been to the South. I wanted to know more about oppression, racism, and the history of Jim Crow. Frankly, not much has changed in America."

"You're telling me! Why do you think I'm over here? There's only an illusion of change. I think about Gunnar Myrdal's *An American Dilemma: The Negro Problem and Modern Democracy*. He talks about America and its colorful constitutional ideals. But that's all they really are, unfulfilled ideals. Jim Crow is alive and kicking in a blue suit, white shirt, and red tie."

"Anthony, where do you go to college and what do you study?" Danielle chimed in.

"I studied sociology and ethnic studies. I graduated from the University of California, Berkeley, and did my graduate work at the University of California, Santa Cruz."

"You seem very passionate about societal change," Gerry said.

"Well, the more I change, the less society does."

"Do you ever relax and just forget about such matters?"

"I relax . . . eat, sleep, listen to jazz, sip wine, jazz. In fact, I'm relaxing right now. Jazz is mental wine."

"You look tired, Anthony," Gerry observed.

"I'm beyond tired. More like beat down, whipped."

"Would you like a massage or something?" Gerry offered.

"That would be nice, but I'm fine. Thanks though."

"Are you sure you don't want a massage, Anthony?" Danielle seduced.

"I just need to chill, take this journey one step at a time."

"Say, Anthony, do you want to come with us to Switzerland for a few days?" Danielle asked.

"Are you serious? Gerry, is she joking?"

"No, she is serious. Danielle would not kid you. Do you want to come home with us?"

"How can I come home with both of you when you live in different places?"

"We are still on vacation, and I am staying with Danielle," Gerry explained.

"That sounds tempting, but I really need to get back to Paris."

"Paris is not going anywhere. Come with us for a few days, see how beautiful Switzerland is," Danielle persisted.

"I'm very flattered, but Paris calls." And I looked at Gerry and Danielle, and heard Duke's mantra: "Never pass up an adventure." In my heart, I knew it would probably be one for the archives. However, my super-ego kept casting long shadows of doubt. Were these broads for real?

"What would we do in Switzerland?" I probed.

"Party, drink, eat good chocolate and *Gschnätzltes*. You could meet some of our friends, and we could take you to the countryside!" Gerry enthused.

"Damn . . . you sure make it hard!"

"It's not supposed to be hard," Gerry contravened.

"Maybe we can persuade you," Danielle suggested sinisterly.

"How do you plan to do that?" my curiosity peaked.

"We can perform for you!" Gerry declared.

"Perform? Perform what? In Amsterdam, I saw some performances."

"You haven't seen everything, Anthony. You haven't seen us naked. Would you like to see?" asked Danielle.

"My eyes are all yours."

"Good. What do you want us to do?"

"Take off your clothes and cakewalk."

I did not think that Gerry and Danielle would do anything. They began to slowly undress. Danielle licked Gerry's nipples and they turned cherry red. Gerry rubbed Danielle's crotch tentatively. Danielle grabbed Gerry's hand and stuffed it into her pelvis. Gerry blushed and hid her other hand beneath Danielle's bra. Danielle flung her head back in ecstasy. She leered at me and licked her tongue over her top lip, very invitingly. Soon, both of them swam in a bucket of nakedness.

I sat back, content to watch, thinking how Duke would berate me for not participating. But I was thoroughly satiated from that thalassic night with Tia.

Italy to Switzerland

Corfu to Italy, now Geneva
I disembark the TGV and trek to McDonalds
A taste of home is desired: fries, coke,
a Quarter Pounder (oops! Royale with cheese)
Brie and baguettes, over-rated and not a meal of
choice
Several hours and Paris will greet me with open
arms
Anticipation for the City of Light gives me
renewed vigor
Home is inside my belly now
Statues impersonating humans,
movements as coins drop in buckets
Jet d'Eau, a large water fountain
Lake Geneva empties into the Rhone River,
From a distance, the water spouts into the air
Two African-Americans stroll the Promenade in
front of me.
Bon jour monsieur et madame!
They stare at me with perplexity.
Parlez-vous français un peu?
Still no reply, where are you from?
I am greeted with smiles.
Where are you from?
We are from Washington DC. You?
Oakland, California.

GERMANY: FIGHTS, HISTORY, AND DECEPTION

Summer, 1998: France finally triumphed over Brazil in the World Cup. I was fortunate enough to have been present. The postgame festivities left one blind in one eye and lame of limb twice.

In the upcoming weeks, I would be touring Germany. According to what others said, Germany lacked a certain cosmopolitanism and diversity. I heard that Munich and Köln were centers of art, culture, and gothic romance. However, I wanted to know about Kassel since I would be mainly staying there. I also heard that various dialects of German posed linguistic barriers from region to region. I was shocked.

Between Frankfurt and Hannover, Kassel was beautifully tranquil. A population of Nigerians by way of Benin, Eritreans, Ethiopians, Turks, Iranians, and Italians resided in Kassel. (I had the best Sicilian ice cream there.) African American expatriates and GI's, as well as an Indian population all co-existed in Kassel.

Located in central Germany, Kassel has a total population of 200,000 or so. It was the home of the renowned folklorists Jakob and Wilhelm Grimm. Kassel is also one of the stops on the German Fairy Tale Road, which stretches from Hanau to Bremen. Additionally, Kassel hosts documenta, the world's preeminent contemporary art exhibition, which takes place every five years.

While in Germany, I had come to learn of Germany's Black Holocaust that took place from 1890-1945. During this period, Germany had colonized large portions of Africa. At the famous

Berlin Conference of 1884-85, Germany had carved up Tanzania, Cameroon, Togo, and Namibia. As early as 1868, German settlers, missionaries, and soldiers besieged Namibia's coast. And in 1884, Germany annexed land, that it later named South West Africa.

Of course, with the signing of the armistice of 1918, Germany lost most of its colonies to France, Great Britain, and the Union of South Africa. Standard historians cite such territorial losses as the spark of World War II. Furthermore, I had heard that the Nazi party had been planned in Tanzania during the inter-war period. According to one account, the word Nazi is a corruption of a Tanzanian word that means coconut. As the story goes, the original architects of the Nazi party consisted of former military men who assembled in Tanzania and fronted as a soccer team, touring the world. The team's logo was a coconut.

In the summer of 1989, Frederic Otomo, a Cameroonian immigrant, who had a run-in with an overly officious subway conductor, was eventually shot and killed by police in Stuttgart. Needless to say, my mind was full of unsettling feelings about Germany. Even the comfort of Hansel's 3,500-square-foot warehouse studio, softened by Miles and Coltrane, rocked by Kate Bush, and smoothed by The Temptations and The Spinners, did not alleviate my anxiety.

Witnessing gangs of Turks who-riding in BMW 325i's, blasting hip-hop, shocked me. Many of them, I was told, professed to be Muslims, and this apparent incongruity reminded me of Yemenites in Oakland selling rotgut, pork, and menthol cigarettes.

Rambling through the center of Kassel, America's hip exports surrounded me. Ice Cube, Snoop Dogg, and the Westside Connection spat from storefronts. Unlike in America, every song was uncut and adult-explicit. Evidently the Germans had no idea of what was being said, the context totally eluded them.

Continuing my stroll, I ran into a guy (about my age) dressed in American attire. Perhaps he was Latino, but he did sport a New York Yankees cap, Timberland boots, and matching FUBU shirt and pants. But when I spoke, motivated by the familiarity of his appearance, I discovered that he was not Latino. Neither was he a GI stationed in Frankfurt. Neither knew he much English. He was Iranian, and I would encounter him again, face to face.

It was a Saturday afternoon, and I was returning to Hansel's studio, having explored the center of town. Along the way I got lost, and bumped into a Ghanaian who spoke English. During our brief conversation, he told me about a place called Da Jam. It was a hip-hop club frequented by folks on Friday and Saturday nights. For whatever reason, Hansel had not mentioned it to me.

Later, that evening, I asked Hansel about Da Jam. He told me that it was just a block up the street. I was curious about why Hansel had never mentioned it. Last night—the night of my arrival—Hansel had taken me to the University of Kassel for a party. There had been no hip-hop there. Nonetheless, I needed a change and was eager to check out Da Jam. Night spread like shadows in the Thuringian Forest. Dressed in jeans, a Pelle Pelle cap, a Karl Kani shirt, and a pair of black Karl Kani boots, the ones with the metal emblem above the shoelaces, I ventured out.

Ahead of me, half a block away, four Turks were harassing an Ethiopian. All of them appearing less than six feet, I found them unimposing, and wondered if my brother had the situation under control. Who did these Turks think they were anyway? I resolved to check it out, but before I could get close enough, two of the Turks accosted me.

"Where in the hell do you think you're going?" one of them asked, full of truculence.

"Do I know you?" I replied sarcastically.

"You need to back the fuck up!" the other warned.

Confounded, I played it coolly, and walked over to the Ethiopian to break up the hem they had him in. But again, I was interrupted; this time by two bouncers who had come outside and told all of us to disperse. Somewhat relieved, I entered the club—I did not want to get in a fist fight my second night in town.

As soon as I got through the door, I ran into the Iranian from earlier on. He looked at me; I looked at him. We started to talk.

"What's up? I'm Anthony."

"What's up? I'm AZ," he replied.

I wanted information on the scene, so immediately I queried AZ. What type of hip-hop was played here? Were the drinks terribly expensive? What was the ratio?

In the process, I learned that AZ had an uncle who lived in Los Angeles, and that he had visited him there several times. AZ was also a friend of a retired GI from Texas, who, in addition to being a DJ at Da Jam, was the proprietor of a shop specializing in hip-hop attire.

"Anthony, what do you do?" AZ asked. "Are you a GI?"

"No, I'm not a GI. Actually, I'm a writer and I've been traveling around Europe for the past three months."

"How do you like Kassel?"

"It's not bad. I'm still adjusting to the culture and people, though. I've only been here one day."

"Do you want a drink?" AZ asked. "It's on me."

"Sure. Cool, but I'll buy the next round."

Da Jam was wide-open, spacious. From where I stood, the DJ booth was to the right, about eight feet above the dance floor, a miniature turret. To the left, all the way across the room, behind a long glass wall, one could find the bar. Neither dark nor smoky, Da Jam had a very chic air: composed as opposed to frenzied.

AZ ordered us both pints of Guinness. Already, I scoped the room for dreamboats. Stepping away from the counter, we saw two Spanish women visiting from Barcelona, and a woman of Turkish descent from Macedonia. Though Greek, she looked thoroughly Latina like those from the Mission (in San Francisco). They asked AZ and me where we were from, and casual talk ensued.

"So, how do you ladies call yourselves?"

"I am Mercedes. This is Sarah, and Alexandra."

"My name is Anthony, and this is AZ."

Before I could decide on what to say next, AZ pulled me aside.

"Anthony, tonight is pussy night," he informed me, out of earshot of our new acquaintances. I stood in awe.

"Yes, believe me. If you tell a woman here that you're from California, you'll probably get laid. These women love men from California. Most of the black guys here are GI's from California, and they get plenty."

I did not reply since my father taught me to believe none of what I hear and only half of what I see. Inasmuch as I was not a GI, and from northern—not southern—California, AZ's advisory seemed erroneous.

But perhaps error worth pursuing because the lasses in the club had ass like sisters in Atlanta—not quite. Alexandra was a stunningly enticing woman. She was maybe five-two, five-three, shapely loins, tanned like copper in tropical sun. Her hair was midnight and eyes topaz, bordering on brown. An amber aura was her amulet.

"Alexandra, would you care to dance?" I asked.

"Yes. I'd love to dance. What took you so long to ask me?"

"I was trying not to be impetuous."

"Anthony, what do you do back in California?"

"I'm a free-lance reporter for an African American daily."

"Are you on assignment in Germany?"

"No, I'm visiting a friend of mine who lives here in Kassel. What about you?"

"I work for an insurance company, but my true love is language. I speak English, Spanish, Turkish, and Greek."

"Impressive! How do you retain all those languages?"

"I don't know. You just get used to it, I guess."

Of course, I should not have been surprised. In Europe, the educated were bilingual, at the very least.

Meanwhile, I Got Five on It by the Luniz, followed by Snoop Dogg's Gin and Juice, packed the floor like Senegambians in the hold of a British frigate. Bodies mashed and mixed in symbiotic grind.

Though Alexandra's eyes are closed, she reaches out and pulls me closer. Accepting her invitation, I absorb her. She responds by mumbling, "Ummmmmmmm." Above her brief delectation and the rotund bass, I hear voices taunting me. But I ignore all, save the sensation of Alexandra's curves carving canyons in my desire. And now my eyes are closed.

When I open them, four Turks surround me, the same ones who had harassed the Ethiopian outside the club. Ignoring them, I continue to dance, until one of the Turks steps in between Alexandra and me.

Déjà vu. Years ago, back home, in Alameda, to be exact, I was with a woman from Yemen in a bowling alley. No less than five of her countrymen rolled up on me and tried to discourage me from enjoying my date. I sucker-punched the biggest one, and the rest bitched out. Later, the woman took me home, fed me, and we jazzed until twilight.

One of the Turks grabbed me by the shoulders in order to push me away from Alexandra. But before his grab took hold, I had knocked his hands off me. Immediately, the other Turks pressed closer.

"You need to stop dancing with her!" one Turk insisted.

"Who are you . . . her father?" I asked sarcastically.

"No, but she is one of us. And she should not be dancing with you!" another Turk steamed.

"Muthafucka, if you ain't her father, her brother, her family, then you need to step the fuck off !" I threatened. Immediately, Mercedes and Sarah ran over and pulled Alexandra away.

The Turks bum-rushed me, but I slumped to the floor and came up behind one of them. With a straight right, I cuffed him on the ear and he hollered. My ring had cut his lobe and blood dribbled on his white shirt. Another Turk tried to sneak a short hook to my ribs, but my fist smashed his jaw and his head shot back. Without hesitation, I flew to him, clamped him between his crotch and around his neck. Picking him off the floor, I dropped him on top of my knee and he fell like lifeless squid. The other two Turks faltered, staring and snorting instead. People scattered and soon the floor was nearly empty. Out of nowhere, AZ jabbed the third Turk in the eye and it swelled like a circus balloon.

"Anthony, let's go," AZ shouted. "We don't want to get arrested over this nonsense."

He did not have to tell me twice. We bounded out of Da Jam in less than one. Outside, AZ unlocked his car and we jumped in. As soon as we turned left out of the parking lot, onto Sanderhauser, the Polizei pulled up behind us. I could not believe it. I was going to jail my second night in Kassel.

AZ pulled over, and complied with the *Polizei*. They asked for ID and automobile registration. Come to find out, they were oblivious to what had just transpired inside the club. Rather, they seemed to be profiling Iranians like AZ. They would not allow AZ to leave until he paid them on the spot. AZ paid the fee for failure to operate a turn signal, and we drove off, evidently not free in Germany.

False Impressions

Frankfort
Mannheim
Koln
Munich
And finally Kassel
Miles Davis, Maxwell, Kate Bush, Coltrane,
and the Spinners
3,500 square foot loft, continental breakfast,
daily
Herculus, waterfalls, the Cascades,
The Black Forest, Black Forest gateau, Black
Forest ham
Cuckoo clocks
Authentic German cuisine (pork!)
Turkish corner stores, reminiscent of Yemen Ma &
Pop
stores back home
BMW-tricked out by Turkish thugs, acting ghetto,
pseudorappers
Selling illegal pharmaceuticals
The best Indian and Italian dining
Fresh Italian ice-cream
Sounds of musical US-everywhere
US Military Men (Are you a GI?)
Natural water springs, drinking from the Well
10:00 pm sunsets, amazing starry nights
Late night strolls in the forest
Japanese salt pools, saunas, and deep body
massages
Pork everywhere! Where's the poulet?

Gypsies, singing and performing,
mysterious mesmerizing movement
Pick-pockets lurking, begging for Deutsche Marks
Clothes, Levis twice the price of a pair of US
jeans
Hansel's loft, a one-stop shop, photography studio,
office, home,
A jewel hidden behind a dingy brick architectural
structure
Freaking at Da Jam
Guest MCing at the club, drinks galore
Harassed by possessive Turkish men
Spanish and Turkish girls intrigued by the badge of
America
Called a Swartz at a Techno Club, no entry
permitted
Kassel

ENGLAND:
BLANDNESS IN BRIXTON

I am in Tottenham, one of London's boroughs to the north, en route to Brixton, where I hope to fathom some of the black scene outside of central London. Tottenham is ethnically diverse and there seems to be a peaceful co-existence among the inhabitants. Afro-Caribbeans, East Indians, Ashkenazi Jews, Turks, and Iranians all live here.

Leaving Evelyn's home—Evelyn is an extended relative of mine from St. Lucia—I walk four blocks south to catch a red double-decker to the Underground. In fifteen to twenty minutes, I arrive at the Oakwood station. People have been telling me that I need to visit Brixton in order to see how blacks live in England. Black people in Brixton do not take any shit, I am further told.

My route shall consist of taking the Oakwood line to the Piccadilly line. At Green Park, I shall catch the Victoria line all the way to Brixton. The trip shall take at least an hour.

Brixton, a vibrant and edgy district south of the River Thames, is approximately 3.3 square miles. It is the home of the Jamaican community in London. Brixton's ethnic identity changed during the 1940s and '50s with the huge influx of West Indian immigrants. So-called inter-racial marriages are frequent in Brixton, being roughly eight times more common than in America.

Concerning employment opportunities and salary earnings, Afro-Caribbean women do better than black men in Brixton. Nonetheless, two out of every three unemployed persons are black, one-third of the housing is sub-standard, and social amenities are next to nil. Still, Brixton annually hosts the Notting Hill Carnival, a multi-cultural experience, attracting over a million and a half people from Britain and around the world, making it the largest street festival in Europe.

In April of 1981 and in September of 1985, Brixton became the scene of major race riots. In the first case, Operation Swamp 81, in which hundreds of black youth were stopped and searched by the police, sparked discontent that led to charred vehicles, including police vans, smashed windows of boutiques, and fleeing TV's and stereos. Then, in 1985, more riots erupted after a police officer (accidentally?) shot and wounded a black woman during a police raid. Ten years later, more cars burned, more shops ransacked, and more bobbies caught brickbats, after the death of a black man in police custody. In 2000, Sir William Macpherson's inquiry into the murder of Stephen Lawrence—a black man stabbed to death by a gang of white youths in April of 1993—acknowledged that the (London) Metropolitan Police still suffered from "institutional racism."

At the heart of Brixton is the market on Electric Avenue, which sells African and Caribbean produce, traditional fruit, vegetables, and fish. The song "Electric Avenue" (1983), written and sung by Eddy Grant, refers to the first shopping street to be lit by electricity—the year was 1888. Grant's lyrics also express the poverty and rage of blacks living in Brixton: "Workin' so hard like a soldier/Can't afford the things on T.V./Deep in my heart I abhor you/Can't get food for the kid."

Former British Prime Minister John Major spent part of his childhood in a two-room flat off Coldharbour Lane, and started his political career as a Lambeth Councillor while still living near Brixton. Former British Prime Minister Harold Macmillan was born in Brixton. David Bowie was also born there, in Stansfield Road. The drum and bass producer Dillinja hails from Brixton. The song "Guns of Brixton" by The Clash, written by Paul Simonon, is an example of the Caribbean and reggae flavor of the area and of its influence on white rock musicians like Simonon.

Former British Prime Minister John Major spent part of his childhood in a two-room flat off Coldharbour Lane, and started his political career as a Lambeth Councillor while still living near

Brixton. Former British Prime Minister Harold Macmillan was born in Brixton. David Bowie was also born there, in Stansfield Road. The drum and bass producer Dillinja hails from Brixton. The song "Guns of Brixton" by The Clash, written by Paul Simonon, is an example of the Caribbean and reggae flavor of the area and of its influence on white rock musicians like Simonon.

Emerging from the Underground, I hear the sounds of a Kirk Franklin version of hip-hop reggae being used as a platform to preach the message of Christianity and the acceptance of Jesus. Pulsating through Cerwin Vega speakers was the music of Chaka Demus and Pliers' "Murder She Wrote," but the words were those of an evangelist. If Kirk Franklin could use funk, rhythm and blues, and hip-hop beats to recruit a generation of youth to the Gospel of Christ, then why should Caribbeans not do the same thing? It was literally dancehall for Jesus.

Entering the market, I met a brother from New York who had been in Brixton for a week hustling bootleg rap movies and tapes. He told me that he had come to London in order to accumulate British pounds, take them back to the States, and exchange them for a higher rate.

While in Brixton, I had every intention of relishing as much Jamaican food and reggae as possible. Evelyn had suggested that I attend a party, or "rave," as she called it; so I milled through the city in search of one for later on. Some pedestrians told me about a place called Brixton Academy. The building in which it was located had been one of the Astoria cinemas. The cinema opened in 1929, but closed down in 1972. In 1983, the cinema was renovated into Brixton Academy, a venue with a capacity of 4,921. Recognized as the largest non-arena venue in London, Brixton Academy regularly attracts big name international acts.

The trek had whetted my appetite and I found myself craving jerk chicken, rice and peas, plantains, ginger beer, and a Red Stripe. I happened upon a place called Takes Two. It was quite small, but the aroma of island life lingered in the air. I walked in and started to case the joint. The ambiance proved easy-going and good-natured.

At the counter, I picked up a menu, and an elderly woman approached slowly, calmly.

"Can I help you, mahn?" she asked with a thick Caribbean-British accent.

"Cheers," I said. "I would like a few minutes to look over the menu."

"Take your time, mahn. No rush."

Each day featured a special dish. Today, it was jerk and curry chicken. Beef and chicken patties were served every day. Beverages ranged from ginger beer and sour sop, to Ting and Red Stripe. Eventually, I ordered jerk chicken, rice and peas, a green salad, and ginger beer.

"Is tat all for you, young mahn? Would you like to try a patty or some plantains?" the elder asked.

"I'll have a side of plantains, please."

"Do you want your jerk chicken extra spicy?"

"That's the only way I can eat it."

"Okay, young mahn. I will make it really spicy for you."

"Thank you very much."

Taking a seat near the window, I watched the people pass by. Besides me, there were only four or five diners in the restaurant. About twenty minutes passed before my food arrived. I prayed and placed my fork into the oblong multi-colored plate. Lifting a full helping to my mouth, I watched the fragrant swirls of steam rise and then disappear. A smile of satisfaction appeared on my face, and the elder woman watched me approvingly.

However, the more I ate, the less I wanted to continue. The rice and peas tasted the same as I had had elsewhere. But the jerk sauce was rather mild, not at all spicy. The jerk in the States, not to mention Jamaica, would put your tongue on fire. It crossed my mind that perhaps the blandness of English cuisine had somehow rubbed off on this food. My plate was still full and I thought about getting up and leaving. But out of respect for the elder woman, I finished almost all of it.

"What do you tink of the food?" she asked, leaving the counter and coming to my table.

"It was great. Not as hot as I would've liked, but tasty nonetheless. You're a great cook."

"Tank you, young mahn."

Of course, I was lying: it was the worst Caribbean food I had ever eaten. "No more West Indian food in London," I resolved. Indian food would be less of a risk. Then I caught my carping and let the matter drop.

When the elder woman brought the check, I could not believe it: twenty-five pounds for some very unsavory dish. I paid, wished the matron good day, and left. Walking down the street, I was wishing for a single monetary unit for all of Europe, thinking that the latter might make London less expensive. But the British were fighting against European unification like a bulldog.

En route to the Underground, I passed a record shop. In front stood a brother from the Nation of Islam. He wore a fine-pressed black suit, white pinpoint shirt, and a burgundy and gold bow tie. His head was shaven bald. He hawked no papers or pies; neither did he squawk a syllable. He struck me as less adamant than any NOI Muslim I had ever seen. Had British blandness rubbed off on him, too?
"As-salaam alaykum," I passed by, greeting him.

"*Wa alaykum as-salaam,*" he returned in a clipped, British accent heavy with glottal stops. He sounded unlike any Muslim I had ever heard. He handed me a flier announcing some protest against the British government's ban of Louis Farrakhan from England. Apparently, British intelligence had threatened to blast Farrakhan out of the sky if he even so much as flew over England.

The store was a mere hole in the wall, but it boasted a wide range of vinyl. I flipped through several dozen records, but nothing stirred me up.

Descending into the Underground, I headed back north.

Brixton Blues

South London
Jamaicans
British Africans,
And Caribbean
The Empire Windrush Ship (492 Jamaicans)
Docked
Brixton comes alive
The dawn of multiculturalism
Windrush Square, 1998 (Memorial),
A Commemoration?
South London
A new start, a new life, the first large group
West Indians immigrants to the UK post WWII
CRL James, writer and black political activist
Vincent van Gogh-Boarding House living Hackford
Road
David Bowie, Let's Dance/Fame-Stansfield Road
The Clash
Sharon Osbourne, Ozzy's belle
Stereo MCs-Acid Jazz
The Adventure of the Three Garridebs-Sherlock
Holmes
Anti-Race Riots
Community Policing
Electric Avenue-
1888, electric lamps, the first to illuminate
World Markets; Afro-Caribbean products
Mild tasting Jerk Chicken
Punk Music- 1977 (yesterday)
The 80s New Romantic Movement

(Eurythmics/Pet Shop Boys)-booked
The Fridge — Africa Centre nights (Soul II
Soul)/Trance Music
The Nation of Islam
Attitude
Where's the festival?

PARIS:
CITY OF LIGHT

London had been unique and burdensome at the same time. The absence of sunshine only exacerbated the situation. And if the latter were not enough, the hassle of juggling a dozen different currencies broke the camel's back.

A week had passed, and I was ready to return to Paris. I looked forward to traveling first-class on the Eurostar. The morning was unusually bright and I could not wait to leave. When I finished re-packing my pack, I went downstairs, said good-bye to Evelyn, and proceeded to the Underground. My trip would consist of taking the Piccadilly line to Leicester Square, where I would transfer, and take the line to Waterloo International Station. There, I would purchase a ticket for the Eurostar.

It was 1:00 P.M. when I arrived at Waterloo. Immediately, I found the queue—which was surprisingly short—and paid 188 pounds or $94 U.S. dollars for a one-way ticket to Paris. The trip would take three hours.

The idea of traveling under the English Channel (known as the Chunnel) excited me. Once aboard, I found my seat and then treated myself to a glass of Riesling. The world seemed aright: the World Cup was underway, "Go-Go-Allez" by Ricky Martin flooded the airwaves, along with Brandy's "The Boy Is Mine." Jennifer Lopez's hit single "If You Had My Love" quickly climbed the charts, and the international community eagerly watched as U.S. President William Jefferson Clinton faced impeachment.

Not only is Paris the capital of France, it is also the capital of the Île-de-France, the territory encompassing Paris and its suburbs. Paris is France's seventy-fifth department (French: *département*). France consists of ninety-seven departments or administrative sectors. The Gross Domestic Product of Paris alone is larger than that of Australia. Along with London, Paris is the financial center of Europe, accounting for more than 30% of France's white-collar population and more than 40% of the headquarters for French corporations. Paris is also home to the largest single business district in Europe, La Défense and, to the second largest stock exchange, with subsidiaries in Belgium, Portugal, the United Kingdom, and the Netherlands.

Known worldwide as the City of Lights, Paris has been a major tourist attraction and destination for many centuries. Renowned for its architecture, museums, cafés, universities, and tree-lined boulevards, Paris sits on the Seine River, which divides the city into the Right Bank to the north and into the smaller Left Bank to the south. Paris was also the capital of France's colonial empire, which stretched over three continents (Africa, North America, and Asia). In short, France consists of Paris and the provinces, that is, Paris and everything else.

When I arrived at Gare du Nord (train station), I noticed that there were no black people working in any capacity. In London, most black people worked as security guards for high-end boutiques like Gucci, Channel, Louis Vuitton, and Hugo Boss. Others drove cabs or worked as bouncers at nightclubs. In Paris, competition for employment has proven stiff for many of France's black immigrants. However, African-Americans have wielded their American status as a shield to protect them from racial hostilities suffered by Africans, Arabs, and West Indians. Of course, those from Maghreb, particularly Algerians, endure the most resentment because of their Islamic faith and successful overthrow of the French following the Battle of Algiers (1954-62).

At the station, I took a cab en route to Aunt Rachel's in Neuilly. Neuilly is a very tony section of Paris. Though located on the outskirts to the west, Neuilly is not suburban in a typically American sense. However, Neuilly proved to be a bastion of decadent wealth and well-groomed snobbery.

We passed Gare de l'Est and followed boulevard de Magenta to Place de la République, where several streets terminated. Picking up rue de Turbigo, we skirted Forum des Halles and the world-famous Louvre. When we came upon the Jardin des Tuilleries, the taxi driver began to question me.

"Monsieur, vous allez à Neuilly, n'est-ce pas?"

"Oui, je vais à Neuilly," I responded.

"Je m'appelle Césaire, monsieur. Je viens de Gabon. Comment vous appelez-vous?"

"*Je m'appelle Antoine.*" Then, for whatever reason, Césaire switched to English.

"What brings you here to Paris?" he asked.

"I'm here on vacation, visiting family and friends."

"Your family lives in Neuilly?" curiosity creased his voice.

"Yes." I paused to marvel at the huge, rose granite Egyptian obelisk that was given to Charles X by the Viceroy of Egypt in 1829. It is the oldest monument in Paris, dating from the thirteenth century B.C.E. On the obelisk are inscribed the deeds of Ramses, but I cannot read hieroglyphics so I cannot tell you what his deeds were.

"So, Césaire, do you drive a taxi for a living, or is this just a part-time situation?"

"I do this until I can get a good job. I have a law degree, but can't get the work I desire here in Paris."

"Why is that? Seems like an intelligent African should be able to get a job here."

"The French do not hire their former colonized subjects. They complain that we take jobs from their countrymen. But are we black Africans who live in France not their countrymen too? From Africa, some of my brothers and sisters go on to the universities in France, England, and America. But when they return from their studies and try to get a good job in France, Paris especially, they have no luck. No one will hire them."

"What do you think is the solution?" I asked.

"There is nothing anyone can do, but pray for an opportunity. Racism and discrimination in this country are very bad. The French still treat us like we are their servants and subjects. There is a serious tension between Africans and the French. To them, we are second-class citizens, much like how your blacks are treated in America."

"That's interesting because, as a tourist here, I receive better treatment when Parisians find out that I'm from the States."

"The only way an African can hope to get an employment opportunity in this country is if he marries a French national or else a woman with French citizenship," Césaire explained.

"Then why not marry one?"

"It's not that easy, brother. *C'est plus difficile que ça.* You have to be the right man or find the right woman for that to happen."

Césaire's comments started me to thinking about the exogamy of black American men marrying white American women. Was the latter a matter of love, or was it socio-political strategy to gain status as the "right" kind of black man? I did notice that many men of African descent were married to French women. And my Aunt Rachel had numerous black American expatriate friends who were married to French men.

Césaire pointed out the Arc de Triomphe to me. It is the world's largest triumphal arch, commissioned in 1806 by Napoleon in honor of his Grande Armée. But, in 1940, the Nazis goose-stepped through the Arc, and Parisians cried a river of tears.

Moments later, we were in Neuilly. I paid Césaire the fare and left him a generous tip. Normally, I do not over-tip, but I appreciated his conversation.

"*Césaire, mon frère, merci beaucoup pour l'entretien.* I learned a few things."

"*C'était mon plaisir. Vous êtes très sympa. Bonne chance, mon frère.*"

Climbing out of the taxi, my mind swirled. A quote from Maya Angelou's "Singin' and Swingin' and Getting Merry Like Christmas" crowded my already giddy mind: "I saw no benefit in exchanging one kind of prejudice for another." I could clearly understand why African-Americans wanted to escape the virulent racial prejudice and hatred of the States. But I could not separate the romance of the City of Lights, its passion for "hot" jazz in the '50s and the miscegenation that started in cafés like the Monaco (where Richard Wright hung out) from the harsh economic discrimination suffered by Césaire and other Africans. Chester Himes, in a letter to Carl Van Vechten, written upon Himes's return from the Gironde region of France, had offered a sobering view of black Americans in Paris: "I didn't get to meet many Negroes in Paris. But I met Williams Gardner Smith, I saw Ollie Harrington, and a few others. They all hang around the Monaco in the shadow of Dick Wright. The real French don't have anything to do with them but take their money . . . To me they seem an unhappy lot. But they swear they love Paris."

Reaching Aunt Rachel's door, I wondered whether I would love Paris or hate it.

Paris en conclusion

Trente ans à obtenir ici
Je suis ici
Je vis un rêve
Les choses sont surréalistes
Je suis intimide-struct_
Lumières partout
Romance dans le ciel
Africains partout?
Français, anglais, espagnol
Amour, exploration,
Je pense à rester et à vivre ici
Je ne peux pas croire que je suis sur le sol
français!
J'ai été amoureux.
Je ne veux pas retourner aux Etats-Unis
Les champions Elysees
Cafés, restaurants, histoire
Mot, Weed, vin, femmes, monde
Josephine, Sidney, Baldwin, Jones,
Himes, et Langston
Maintenant je
Je vis ici un rêve

Paris, Finally

Thirty years to get here
I am here
I am living a dream
Things are surreal
I am awe-struck
Lights everywhere
Romance in the air
Africans everywhere?
French, English, Spanish
Love, exploration!
I think about staying and living here
I can't believe I am on French soil!
I have fallen in love.
I don't want to return to the United States
The Champs Elysees
Cafes, restaurants, history
Word, weed, wine, women, world
Josephine, Sidney, Baldwin, Jones,
Himes, and Langston
Now me
I am here living a dream

PORTUGAL: ALIVE IN LISBON

This is my last day in Madrid, and I am ready to quit this landlocked city. I have been here for several days, and the visit has proven sufficiently pleasant. Madrid is a classical jewel tucked in a medieval safe.

Tours of museums and colossal buildings dating from the seventeenth century leave me drained. Everything, now, begins to look the same and every new acquaintance hails from California. I had expected hospitality, but hard stares and rudeness greeted me. Being a black man in the heartland of Spain is no Freedman's paradise.

After a few hours in Madrid, I had concluded that no one here had ever seen a black man. But, of course, there have been men of my ilk in Madrid before me. But, as in the States, more blacks live in the coastal and southern regions.

Both Toldeo and Ávila are situated about an hour and a half outside of Madrid: Toledo in Castile-La Mancha, Ávila in Catile-León. I shall miss Toledo, the "city of the three cultures" the most. The narrow maze of streets and its gated walls locked my heart. But the nine caliphal vaults of the Mosque of Cristo de la Luz, built in 999, freed my soul. And forever, the crenellations of Ávila shall remind me of medieval arrows and hot pots of oil.

There was something majestic about traveling back in time. The inhabitants of Spain were blessed to live in the midst of such history. Many of the people in the central mountain range led a very quiet and simple life. I suppose their geographical isolation had much to do with it.

I snapped some great photos, sipped such Moorish drinks as Rose Petal Liqueur, Aromatic Herb Liqueur, and Iced White Rum with Blood Oranges. I conversed with Zaryab about how he introduced asparagus into Al-Andalus, and debated Averroes on the subject of the world's eternity. Averroes insisted that the world is eternal, that the Creator is neither simultaneous with nor prior to the world in time or in causation. I insisted that God created the world in six days, and therefore must have stood in the river of time.

Later, I found myself wandering around the Alcázar, Toledo's most formidable landmark. It had been a fortress of Goths, Muslims, and Christians (in that order). Each of these cultures had rebuilt the Alcázar in their own style; thus it was an architectural palimpsest. But the last incarnation, built by Carlos V, was razed and largely reduced to rubble because the Republicans had bombed out the Fascists, who were ensconced there during the Civil War.

Mountain ranges, rivers, and rich rolling valleys surround Toledo. It abounds with aromatic plants, game, and rockroses—all of which makes it a garden of plenty. Having been conquered by the Romans, the Visigoths, the Christians, and more notably the Moors—who left a strong imprint—Toledo possesses a rich, varied history. I enjoyed roaming the narrow, cobblestone streets, lounging al fresco at the cafés, and eating fruit from the outdoor markets. In the Plaza de Zocodover, I sampled some of the local sandwiches and had tapas galore. The museums and other historic attractions exhausted me though. With the exception of the Museum of Santa Cruz and the El Greco House, everything began to look and feel the same.

About seventy miles outside of Madrid (an hour and fifteen minutes by train) sits Avila, the capital of the province of Avila. At an altitude of 1,127 meters, Avila is the highest provincial capital in Spain. Built in 1085, it is known as the best-preserved walled city in the world, with walls averaging 33 feet in height and 10 feet thick. There are 90 towers and 9 gateways. Even the cathedral in Avila resembles a fortress more than a place of worship.

The view of Avila from Los Curator Postes, an observation post on the Salamanca Road outside the city, is awesome. Nestled above the Adaja River and sheltered by the Gredos Sierra, Avila bewitches the unsuspecting observer.

I had a much better time in Toledo and in Ávila. The people seemed more polite and animated. The food was great, especially the trout from the Tormes River, so remarkably seasoned—along with large helpings of vegetables and yemas de Santa Teresa (a sweet made with egg and sugar), I ate like a king.

Eliza and I are at Atocha Station in Madrid to purchase tickets for Lisbon, Portugal. We arrived about 6:30 P.M. The station is very busy, and the inefficiency of the Spanish rails has made me anxious once again. I take a number, and surmise that we will have to wait at least an hour before getting to the counter. But Eliza's upbeat energy and unflagging optimism still me. She is the perfect travel companion.

I met Eliza in Madrid upon my arrival at Atocha Station a week ago. Ever since, we have been traveling together, depending upon each other for moral support and company. Eliza speaks Spanish and I am her aegis against danger. Like me, she is also from the Bay Area. Without Eliza, I would have been lost, cheated out of my drawers by the Spaniards.

Eliza is twenty-five years old, smart and beautiful, as well as a hustler. She is also politically aware, and quite sensitive to racial and social injustices. Originally from San Francisco, Eliza has just earned her B.A. in Environmental Studies from the University of London, as part of an exchange program. Presently, she is touring the Continent on an Europass. Although the latter limits her travel to France, Germany, Italy, Spain, and Switzerland, within a window of two months, Eliza has already been to the Netherlands, Austria, and Hungary on the same pass. And, in a few hours, she shall be accompanying me to Portugal.

Moreover, Eliza's Europass requires her to record the times and dates of travel, not to mention the countries traveled to, which are supposedly limited to five. However, Eliza forges the pass by erasing times, dates, places, and rewriting them. She has never been caught. I have a three-month Eurail Saverpass that allows me to visit seventeen countries with unlimited travel privileges. Being over the age of twenty-six, I was forced to buy first-class tickets. In many ways, first-class is better. Usually, I have a bed, maybe two, and a private toilet. Also, I have a cabin all to myself.

After an hour or so, our number is finally called, and Eliza marches to the counter to purchase our tickets for Lisbon. I front her the money and she makes the transaction, since I do not know how to ask for two, one-way tickets for a cabin with two beds and a toilet. We are lucky because Eliza secured the last available cabin. Our train is scheduled to arrive at 9:00 P.M. But, in Spain, 9:00 means 9:45, so we have plenty of time.

By now, we are both hungry, and decide to get something to eat. However, Eliza is a vegetarian, so finding something for her is going to be tricky. To our good fortune, she is not a vegan.
"Anthony, are you hungry?" Eliza asked me.

"A bit," I replied.

"I'm starved. If I don't eat soon, I'll pass out. I'm hypoglycemic. I have to eat something fast," she sounded alarmed. Admittedly, I started to get nervous myself.

"Okay. Let's find you some food. What do you want to eat?"

"A cheese sandwich is fine for the moment. I could probably eat some fruit too."

"No problem. I'll get it. Just sit down and rest yourself."

"Thanks. You're great, Anthony."

Atocha is a huge station, but it is hard to find vegetarian food. I see a Pizza Hut and McDonald's. I order Eliza a Quarter Pounder® with cheese (lettuce, tomatoes, onions, and pickles) minus the quarter-pound and a bottle of water. Upon my return, Eliza's face lights up. She takes the sandwich with one hand, unwraps and devours it. Her appetite delights me; usually, women demur in their hunger.

"How is it?"

"It'll do. It's not like the ones at home, but my body needs nourishment," she spoke softly.

"Is there anything else I can get you? If you need anything else, don't hesitate to ask."

"I'm fine Anthony."

While Eliza eats, I read a magazine until our train arrives. But my reading is continually interrupted by thoughts that the train might be ridiculously late or else canceled. But Eliza is relaxed, satisfied, flashing a smile every now and then.

At 9:40 P.M., we board the train and find our cabin. It has bunk beds, adjacent windows, a small icebox, a toilet, and sink. We place our backpacks on the floor, wedging them between the door and the bunk beds.

Thoughts of the World Expo, St. George's Castle, the beaches of Cascais, and the entire Costa Azul excite me. I see naked bodies blazing in the sun. But nine hours of train rain upon me.

"What do you want to munch on?" I asked Eliza.

"You could get us some potato chips, cookies, and beer," she suggested.

I pull out my money to see how much change I have. As it turns out, I have just enough for snacks. I don my shoes, a sweater, and walk two compartments to the rear. In the food car, I order some beers, a few bags of chips, cookies, a veggie and a chicken sandwich. While I wait for the sandwiches, I figure out how to convert pesetas to escudos. The two are close in value. I make the conversion.

"*Hola, señor*! *Buenas noches. Cuánto cuesta*?" I inquired in my best Spanish.

"It will cost you thirteen dollars for everything," the clerk said in passable English, surprising me.

"You speak English?" I asked.

"Yes, I studied in London," he explained.

"Well, thanks for speaking in English. My Spanish is terrible. *Muchas gracias*."

"You are welcome. *Buen viaje*. Goodbye," the clerk said.

Back in the cabin, Eliza is lying on the top bunk writing in her journal. Quietly, I put the snacks away, beer in the fridge, save one. Before I finish my beer, Eliza stops writing, leans over the bunk, and peers at me. Her attention comforts me.

"Hey, did you find everything okay? How was your Spanish?" she asked in English.

"Things actually went well. For the first time, I found someone who spoke English. The food clerk studied English in London. It was nice to finally hear my native tongue."

"Tell me what you got!"

"Wouldn't you like to know?" I teased.

"Come on, tell me."

"Only if you come down here and give me a hug."

"Okay. I'll hug you."

She climbs down and we embrace for several minutes. Her body loosens in my arms. Erotic thoughts grind my mind. Eliza rubs the flat of her palms over my chest. I nibble her ear. Her nipples tickle my ribs. I draw back. Eliza pulls forward.

For twenty minutes or so, we kiss. I am on the ride, and my stomach falls from under me, every other second or so. Eliza's amber browns freeze me. Id tells me to release, but Ego warns against extreme advance. I ask Eliza what she wants from me.

"I want you to be here," she said. "I want you to be gentle with me tonight. My body is craving attention."

"I'm here with you. My body desires your touch, too," I whispered.

"Anthony, kiss me. Give me your hands. Put them where I can really feel you. Yes. Right there!"

"Anywhere you like."

The ante meridian came fast, and when I checked the time, it was two o'clock. For the past several hours, Eliza and I have been at the carnival. We rode the double-backed beast and roller-coasted up and down. I swam through the tunnel of love. Eliza saddled me tightly all the way to Lisbon.

Around nine, the train pulled into Santa Apolonia station and I pulled out of Eliza. The sun spilled pristinely, and the mercury hovered above one hundred and ten. It was so hot that the devil was upset.

Eliza seemed very excited to be in Portugal. She got up, rubbed her eyes, and gave me a short, but juicy kiss. I felt connected to her. If physical intimacy is a shortcut to getting to know someone, then Eliza and I were well acquainted.

Disembarking from the train, we ran into more Californians. These women were from Sacramento. They were students at Sacramento State, and like us they were in search of lodging in Lisbon. Once inside the station, we pulled out our copies of *Let's Go Europe* and of *Lonely Planet*. We cross-referenced hostels and discussed our options. Terry and Marissa had heard about a hostel on the north side of town, located in an old building with ten stories and no elevator. A British family, eager to grease young tourists, owned it.

Terry and Marissa had a detailed map of the city, and we all studied it intently. We figured that the walk from the station to the hostel would take about thirty minutes. Maybe the trip was only fifteen minutes by taxi or bus. Whatever the case, it was too damn hot to walk.

We found a bus that ran the length of Rúa Aurea, which paralleled Rúa dos Franqueiros. Rúa dos Franqueiros intersected Avenido da Liberdade, our point of transfer. We were there in ten minutes.

The hostel turned out to be a building that was originally designed as a tenement. In reality, it bore no resemblance to the descriptions in *Lonely Planet* and in *Let's Go Europe*. But good backpackers make the best of any situation, and all of us were seasoned backpackers. So we climbed six stories, met the host, and each party paid for a week in advance. The sixth floor felt like the inside of a blast furnace. Sweat poured down my face like monsoon rain.

Terry and Marissa, Eliza and I settled into our respective rooms. By the time I had undressed to take a nap, it was already noon. Upon awakening, several hours later, I suddenly realized that I was in a country that had in many ways inaugurated the Trans-Atlantic slave trade. Well before Columbus sailed the ocean blue, the Portuguese had been conducting nautical enterprises along the coast of Africa and into the Atlantic. Prince Henry the Navigator equipped these voyages from Lagos, Portugal. In fact, Elmina Castle, the oldest and largest in West Africa, erected by the Portuguese in 1482, served as a garrison and a storehouse for linen and palm oil, earthenware, salt, and ivory, not to mention gold and slaves. As early as 1462, the Portuguese were bringing gold and slaves back to Europe in ever-increasing numbers. Until the Dutch siege of 1637, Elmina (located near the Benya River in present-day Ghana) had remained under Portuguese control.

Queen Nzinga (1583-1663) of the Mbundu battled with her warriors against the rapacious Portuguese and their plundering of black slaves in Angola. Of course, there is the famous story of how Nzinga—whose title *ngola* was misunderstood by the Portuguese to be the name of the country, thus *Angola*—went to Luanda to meet the Portuguese governor. Upon entering the room, Nzinga observed that the only seat belonged to the governor. With adroitness and perfect timing, Nzinga summoned one of her attendants, who bent on her knees and became the queen's "seat." From the outset, the governor was outwitted and Nzinga negotiated a treaty with the Portuguese, however brief.

Then, my mind shifted and I had a great desire to see the blacks who lived in Portugal. Where did they reside? What did they look like? What kind of culture(s) had they developed? What languages did they speak? Where did they come from? Were they culturally integrated or assimilated? How much mixing occurred between them and the whites? How would I be treated inasmuch as I had yet to see anyone who looked like me?

I fought with myself over these questions. Then, I remembered something a friend had said. He had exhorted me to follow the unbeaten paths, to speak to the elders, and to befriend the natives so as to become aware of their customs and taboos. He encouraged me to discover ways to blend in, if possible. But my thoughts kept coming back to the meaning of blackness in Europe. I took out my journal and started writing. Immediately, it became clear to me that the residue of centuries of enslavement and cultural whitewashing had predisposed me to fawn over Europe's museums, monuments, and other historic attractions. Here I was in Lisbon having an inner struggle. As W.E.B. Du Bois said, I was feeling my twoness: "two souls, two thoughts, two unreconciled strivings; two warring ideals in a dark body, whose dogged strength alone keeps it from being turn asunder." I did not expect Terry, Marissa, or Eliza to understand what I was feeling, so I kept it to myself.

Night fell like curtains of heavy azure. People spilled in the streets. I decided against going out. I resolved to save my money for day-trips to St. George's Castle and to the Alfama quarter where Saracen architecture prevails. I was eminently excited to see historical examples of Moorish influence and dominance in Europe.

Unbeknownst to me, Eliza was downstairs in the lounge conversing with other guests. When I came upon her, she looked as if to say, "Get me out of here—soon!" I figured that we could explore the numerous shops and restaurants along our block. Without persuasion, Eliza joined me and we were on our way.

The next morning Terry and Marissa awoke bright and early. They knocked on our door, and standing in the hallway, asked us if we wanted to accompany them to St. George. Eliza stroked me and I yelled, "Yes, of course." About an hour later, the four of us convened in the lobby, trying to determine how to get to St. George.

"Anthony, it is way too hot out here for us to walk from here to St. George," Eliza complained.

"What do you suggest we do?" I retaliated.

Before Eliza could reply, Marissa interrupted, "I agree with Eliza. We should take a bus." So we took a bus. The ride lasted less than ten minutes. By the time we alighted, the temperature would seem to have risen fifty degrees.

Narrow cobblestones snaked beneath high, mortar walls. Without end, the cobblestones wound uphill. We found ourselves in the middle of a plaza, where we decided to idle, drink Iced Coffee Liqueur-Lemon Punch and Moscato Cocktails. We also ate ice cream.

The sun continued to sire heat, and we agreed it was time to make the final leg to St. George. Foreground with the castle was a bridge reminiscent of San Francisco's Golden Gate. Actually, this bridge rivaled the latter in every aspect of structural design and charm. Inside, we explored every nook, niche, and quoin. After the Moorish siege of Lisbon in 1147, King Dom Alfonso Henriques had the royal residence moved into St. George's Castle.

Though the castle, like the bridge, was impressive, I desired to see where the blacks hung out. At a distance of about ten city blocks (from the castle), we found a community of Africans. They hailed from Guinea Bissau, Angola, Brazil, and Mozambique. I wondered how many Muslims were amongst them.

As we continued our stroll through this tiny village of sorts, Eliza began to complain of sunburn. Terry and Marissa had applied copious amounts of sun block formulas and seemed uncooked, but RA roiled Eliza.

Conflicted, I accompanied Eliza back to the hostel where I rubbed her down with cold towels and aloe cream. I would have to wait for Terry and Marissa to tell me about the blacks of Lisbon.

Portugal Ambivalence

1998, the World Expo
Castle of Sao Jorge,
I remember the hike, the trek
104 degrees, death heat, endless
Bottles of water galore
European sunburns, heat darken already tanned
skin
Cold Atlantic Ocean Water,
Sangria extreme, illusionary relaxation
Makeshift hostels, 18 floor hikes,
Unstable elevators
Caution, suspicion
Sleeping on white sheets, no covers
Over-populated, over-booked, over-sold
Accommodations
Brits controlling the flow of currency
Too many backpackers
Smells of archaic Moorish living,
711 A.D. conquest
Black Africans hailing from North Africa
Almoravid and Amohade Dynasties
Warring Free Africans
Modern-Lisbon
Broken communities
Mozambique, Angola, Guinea Bissau,
Queen Nzinga
Liberation
Prince Henry domination
Columbus conspiracy
Restauradores Square

Vasco da Gama Bridge (symbols of wealth)
Ribatejo- Arabian horses and black bulls
Little Africa goes unnoticed
Brazilian lives of poverty
Pseudo-Portuguese living
Slavery, isolation, cultural reinvention
Sugarcane plantations
Palmares- (home)
Quilombo sanctuaries
Romantic, isn't it?

SPAIN:
SANTIAGO DE COMPOSTELA

Portugal bejeweled my memory. Even the World Expo—boring as it was—impressed me. I can still see the spectacular view of Lisbon and the ocean from the Castelo de São Jorge (St. George's Castle). I can still feel the heat emanating from Eliza's sunburn, too.

Since meeting in Madrid, it seemed like Eliza and I had been traveling together for the entire summer, though we had only been to Portugal together. Now, we were headed to Santiago de Compostela, located in Galicia, a region tucked away in the northwest corner of Spain. From Lisbon, the train would travel north through Coimbra, Porto, and Viana do Castelo, where it would head east from the Costa Verde, cross the Rio Minho, and enter Spain.

Santiago de Compostela was founded in 813 when, according to legend, a tomb containing the remains of the apostle St. James was discovered in the area. Soon, the city became one of Christianity's great holy sites. Many Christians believed that, making the arduous journey to Santiago's cathedral would halve their time in purgatory. Consequently, so many visitors journeyed to Santiago that the monks had to build monasteries that could host the countless pilgrims en route. As a result, Europe had known its first large-scale travel industry.

Today, Santiago has an estimated population of 92,339, and is known as the "European City of Culture." In fact, the entire old town of Santiago has been designated as a national monument. Still, thousands of Christians make the pilgrimage there, from all over Europe. Some walk, some bike, some even come on horseback or donkey. Of course, there are others, like Eliza and I, who visit for non-religious reasons.

While Eliza busily consulted her copy of *Lonely Planet*, searching for lodging in Santiago, I peered out of the cabin window. And, to my surprise, way up on a hill, there was graffiti on a wall honoring the rap icon Ice Cube, and next to Cube's name appeared the famous words of Malcolm X: "By any means necessary." Not only was I surprised to see native knowledge of Ice Cube and of Malcolm X, but also to see this graffiti in English.

At 7:00 P.M., the train crept into the station on Rúa do General Franco. Eliza had found a place called Hospedaje Santa Cruz, located in the center of town, on Rúa do Vilar, 42, 2nd floor. It boasted newly renovated rooms with huge windows overlooking Santiago's most popular street. After nearly ten hours on the train, both of us desired stationary calm and sleep. Needless to say, we left the station posthaste.

Given Eliza's keen sense of direction, we set out on foot. We passed numerous shops full of medieval relics and curios. Of course, icons of St. James on wooden panels and on mosaics dominated the shop windows. There were also suits of armor. Breastplates, helmets with visors, and gauntlets were being sold singly. However, the swords caught my attention. I wanted to purchase a replica of King Arthur's Excalibur, of which I saw several. There were also Uther Pendragons, pirate cutlasses, Cleopatra daggers, Templar Knights, and Gladius short swords.

Though the quaint granite streets had whetted my exploratory humors, the call of Morpheus proved stronger. So, after checking into Hospedaje Santa Cruz, Eliza ventured out, and I dozed off. African drums, djimbés, cracked a syncopated whip on the wind's back and the wind wailed in a trance. Men in crocodile masks and women in raffia skirts danced up a cloud dust and then disappeared behind it. I woke up to find Eliza staring out the window. Getting out of bed, I loafed toward her. She met me half way with a curt, but wet kiss.

"How was your siesta?" she asked lovingly.

"It was well-deserved. I'm content. How was your exploration?"

"It was good. Santiago has many treasures."

"Such as?"

"Well, I saw some *tunas*."

"Tuna? You mean fish?"

No, of course not. Though, I'm sure there is tuna at the open-air market, but it was closed," Eliza explained.

"So what are *tunas*?" I asked rubbing my eyes.

"*Tunas* are dance troupes that dress in medieval outfits and sing ribald songs. One of the guys even serenaded me."

"Really?"

"Really."

"What did he say?"

"I understood him to say that I was more beautiful than Dulcinea del Toboso."

"Don Quixote's girlfriend?"

"Exactly," Eliza replied, smiling childishly.

"Do you hear those drums out there?" I asked.

"Yes."

"Where's it coming from?"
"There's a group of students in the plaza drumming."

"Do you want to go see?"

"Why not!" piped Eliza.

After performing minor ablutions down the hall, I got dressed and we left. Crossing Rúa Vilar, we followed the sound, paying no attention to the names of streets. We ended up in a sand-filled plaza bearing little green, where young and middle-aged drummers sported blond(e) and brunet(te) dreadlocks, not to mention cowry shell necklaces and bracelets. Some even wore dashikis. All over the city, people were participating in a festival celebrating the expulsion of the Moors. On January 2, 1492, the Moorish general Abu Abdi-Llah, otherwise known as Boabdil, had surrendered to the Spanish, and the Moors were forthwith expelled from Spain. Pockets of Moorish resistance lingered in places like the mountains surrounding Granada, but for little more than a century.

Bewilderment besieged me. Eliza offered looks of sympathy. All of the drummers were white—Spanish, I supposed. I could not ascertain whether they drummed for the Christians or for the Moors. And, if, for the Christians they played, then did why did they adopt the instruments, the dress, and the hairstyle of Africans or blacks in order to do so? It seemed very peculiar, to me, for these Spaniards to be commemorating the defeat of the Moors on African drums. Stranger still was that one gentleman played a five-string lute; a Moor named Zaryab, who had arrived in Al-Andalus in 822, had added a fifth string to the lute. Before Zaryab, the four-string lute corresponded to the four bodily humors: blood, yellow bile, phlegm, and black bile or melancholy. Zaryab had introduced a fifth string to represent the soul.

Compelled to learn more of this drumming and strumming, I approached various drummers in the circle. To my dismay, none of them spoke English. I turned to ask Eliza if she would intercede and translate my questions to them. But she was dancing, rapt by the music, and I feared that the answers to my questions were already painfully obvious.

We spent several days in Santiago, visiting the open-air market, where we bought a basket and filled it with an assortment of cheeses and fruit, and combing the shops. On the third day, we followed Rúa do Vilar and it led us directly to the cathedral. Approaching it, we stood for a moment and marveled at the two Baroque towers that soared over the city. Inside, in the Pórtico de la Gloria, a bejeweled bust of St. James winked at us. Beneath the high altar, in a silver coffer, St. James's remains lounged in Spanish Romanesque splendor. However, what struck me most was on the other side of the cathedral: a statue of Mary holding Baby Jesus and clubbing a demon.

On the fifth day, Eliza and I made our way back to the train station. En route, we stopped at a shop featuring swords, and I bought a replica Excalibur. Walking down Rúa do General Franco, I imagined myself Boabdil pursuing crusaders and pierced the heart and loins of many. Eliza and other pedestrians eyed me curiously, but I paid them no attention.

Before sunset, we finally boarded the train, in search of Basques.

Santiago de Compostela

The Way of St. James the Apostle
El Camino de Santiago, the Pilgrimage
A Medieval route to an ancient cathedral
Tucked away in Northwestern Spain
They come from everywhere
Whether on foot, donkey, horseback, or bicycle
People travel a presumed spiritual terrain
Independent-Galicia
A golden oasis, a City of Culture
A ploy for attracting bodies to a city
For international socio-economic growth
Irish pubs, Guinness stouts, great debates
Unexpected friendships
Bohemians
African djimbes, holistic circles
Frequent encounters with watered down
Rasta wanna-bees
Europeans with dread-locks
Chance meetings with brothas who speak no
English
A conscious reminder of Bay Area living
Thoughts of Berkeley and Santa Cruz haunt my
psyche
Ritual dances, celebratory attire don the
entertainment
Celebration of Moorish dissipation
Food, drink, parties, excitement non-stop
Countless swords and dagger shops
I indulge, I partake, I watch
No English except in the Irish pubs

I flash as many photos as possible
I find a hidden sanctuary
A hotel, an upgrade from a hostel
I reflect, contemplate, and give thanks
Another day, another history lesson
It's time to sleep
I shall explore more tomorrow
After an inexpensive Galician breakfast

SPAIN:
SAN SEBASTIÁN (DONOSTIA)

The fact of being the only black in Santiago de Compostela unnerved me. I consoled myself by thinking that perhaps my presence somehow benefited the local people. Whatever the case, the trip was another adventure, and perhaps its lesson would unfold in the right season.

I did not look forward to our train ride to San Sebastián. The trains in Spain are old and move like arthritic dinosaurs. At times, they get stuck on mountainous inclines, and the time of travel seems to triple. Barring such an incident, this trip would take a full day. Furthermore, I did not look forward to the dingy bathrooms or to the walking chimneys that would be puffing away. However, if I could survive the train ride, then I would enjoy San Sebastián.

Bordering southwestern France, San Sebastián is home to the Basques. I wanted to absorb the local culture and to frequent the beach. San Sebastián would be the last jaunt before Eliza and I headed back to France.

Before the train pulled into Estacion del Norte, countless hours had passed. The local time was 9:15 P.M. I promptly woke up Eliza, who had slept the entire trip. Quickly, we collected our bags and disembarked. A warm, salty breeze greeted us, and the horizon blushed like a bowl of sangria.

As we stood in front of the station, trying to ascertain our bearings, an elderly woman approached us. She asked if we needed lodging for our stay in San Sebastián. I did not understand a word she said, but Eliza did, and spoke to her. The woman had a peculiar accent, different from the Spanish I had heard thus far. I figured her tongue to be Basque.

Since some Americans in Santiago had informed Eliza and me of an upscale hostel where most travelers to this region stayed, we decided to explore this option first. Eliza communicated the latter to Señora Ruiz—Eliza had learned her name—and we left on foot in search of the hostel, which fortunately happened to be only a few blocks from the train station. Unfortunately, the hostel was overbooked, and we hurriedly returned to the station, hoping to find Señora Ruiz. We found her in the same spot, and discovered that she had not found any lodgers. Eliza made the arrangements and we followed Señora Ruiz home.

She led us to a bus stop and paid our fare. We alighted in front of a high-rise apartment building. Señora Ruiz told Eliza that the beach was only a five-minute walk away. Señora Ruiz lived on the 18th floor. We followed her from the elevator to her apartment door. When Señora Ruiz opened it, a house full of Californians (from Los Angeles, San Diego, and San Jose)—we soon discovered—greeted us.

Following brief introductions, Señora Ruiz showed us our room. I told Eliza that I wanted to go to the beach and walk the boardwalk, since I wanted to feel like I was in Spain, not back in California. She agreed to meet me in twenty minutes or so in front of the building.

Señora Ruiz had the most spectacular view that I had seen in Spain. It was 180 degrees of the Rio Urumea (which splits San Sebastián in two, as the Seine does Paris), of lovely beaches, of broad boulevards, and of ornate buildings as far as the eye could see.

San Sebastián, called Donostia in Basque, is the capital city of the province of Guipúzcoa, in the Basque Country. Basque Country (called Euskadi in Basque, País Vasco in Spanish) is an autonomous community within Spain whose capital is Vitoria (Basque: Gasteiz). It is part of the larger Basque native lands, which are also called the "Basque Country." Basque or Euskara is the language spoken by the Basque people. The country is made up of several provinces that include Álava, Vizacava, and Guipúzcoa (of which San Sebastián or Donostia is the capital). San Sebastián's population is roughly

178,017. Located in the northeast region of Spain, along the bend of the Bay of Biscay, San Sebastián's picturesque coastline makes it a popular beach resort.

When Eliza exited the building, we strolled, arm in arm, under countless stars, to the beach. The wind whispered blissfully on our faces. We held hands; every other step, Eliza fizzed like *txacoli*. The white sand was luminescent over our feet.

About a hundred yards down the beach, we came upon a ragged tent. In front of it a young man and woman argued back and forth in English. Both looked forlorn. My heart jumped inside my shirt.

"Hey! Are you okay over there?" I asked.

"Yeah. A-Okay. We're going to stay on the beach tonight. We couldn't find a place to stay. We've been looking for hours without any luck."

I felt bad for this fellow and his belle. But what could we do? Maybe Señora Ruiz knew of another place where they might stay.

"Where are you from, dude?" I inquired.

"I'm from Oakland."

"You're kidding, right? I'm from Oakland, too," I explained.

"No joke. I live near Park Boulevard, several blocks up the street from Oakland High School. On Trestle Glen, to be exact."

"You definitely live in the Oakland," I conceded.

I wanted to keep talking, but sensed that he wanted to be left alone with his girl. Besides, Eliza was pulling on my sleeve. However, I did not want to leave without giving this guy my information. So I gave him the number to our hostel, and Eliza and I ventured off, toward the boardwalk. We walked to the end and sat down. Kicking our legs over the edge, we watched the gibbous moon shimmer luminous booty over the Cantabrian Sea. After a few hours spent launching tranquil vessels, we returned to our room at Señora Ruiz's. At the dining room table, Señora Ruiz and a couple of the Californians were speaking Spanish, laughing, and drinking a fizzy wine called *txacoli*.

The next day, the sun burned a hole in the sky, and it was hotter than Mercury's July. Politics, circumlocutions of globalism, academic acrobatics, and philosophical cogito-ergo-sum's would be left to die. Thalassic odalisques blew sirens in my ear and bronze treasures of nude pirated my Puritanism. But, instead of participating, I would observe in shades and khaki shorts. Admittedly, I harbored serious reservations about being naked amidst strangers. Eliza, to the contrary, seemed more than comfortable to exhibit her sensuality in public purview.

For four magnificent days, Eliza and I lounged in the white sand lapped by the Cantabrian Sea. I only went so far as to doff my tank top, but Eliza went completely nude more than once. Rubbing sunscreen on her back, I noticed how deeply tan she had become. And the more she tanned, the happier and more ebullient she became. The sun not only opened up her pores, but also released the Bohemian in her, heretofore unseen by me. I wanted to spend more time with her, but our separation was imminent.

As the TGV sped through Montpellier and Bordeaux, I could not take my eyes off of Eliza. Heaviness bore down on her newly copper face. At any moment, I expected tears, yet none dropped.

The train arrived at Gare Montparnasse a few minutes after eight. We gathered our belongings, disembarked, and sauntered through the station. Hordes of passengers pressed the corridors, blitzed the benches, and attacked the ticket booths. Eliza had plans to remain in Paris for a few days, before returning to London. Aunt Rachel's, in Neuilly, awaited me.

"Anthony, since this is our last night together, what do you want to do?" Eliza asked.

"I would love to spend some time with you. We could find a hotel, eat, talk, and enjoy each other until sunrise."

"I'd love that, Anthony."

"Then, *allons-y!*"

We flagged a taxi in front of the station, and I told the driver to head toward Montmartre, figuring that we would get a few drinks at Hayne's, before finding a room. I had a strange feeling that we would never see each other again. But the night scintillated with stars and a crescent moon. Calm descended easily over us, and Eliza reached out for me in the back seat.

Without pause, we kissed all the way across the Seine.

San Sebastian Bay

One more day of beauty
Delectable weather, beautiful people
A moment steeped in time
My heart wandered about all I didn't explore
I traveled impulsively to a place I'd only hear about
in name
No prior studies, reading, or tales could have
prepared me
for such wonderment
I felt a connection to a place that connected not to
me
Was it language barriers, distance of place and
time,
or a fear of opening myself?
My companion danced and lived the moments,
completely free
Perhaps her command of Spanish awarded her
linguistic
liberation, an inside pass
I reflected, contemplated,
and analyzed every nuisance with impeccable detail
I spoke very little Spanish, if any
Perhaps I lost the moments,
paralysis captured my dominion, I froze in time
San Sebastian Bay marveled my mind
It took the stress of America away
Ocean smells, free-spirited people, and honest souls
Summer seemed to relax everyone
Siestas were their weapon of choice
Take a nap in mid-day, work later and party

I guess they had centuries to get it right
1014 AD is a long time to be around
It was time to venture back north to Paris
My TGV awaits

PARIS:
HONOR AND RESPECT

Europe afforded me a kind of anarchical freedom wherein I could break the shackles of civil normality as prescribed by both Black and White intellectual life in America. Caught between rebellion and eroticism, I indulged my impulses and allowed them to dance off the wall. This freedom derived from not being psychologically ensnared in the arbitrary constructs of physiognomy, religious affiliation, and politics. In the States, these ideological vises squeezed me into perverse moods of isolation and loneliness. But to laugh, to cry, to self-express, and to think without fear of reproach changed my inner-spirit. I was living more fully inside of my humanity. However, I feared that upon my return to America these intimations of self-sovereignty would simply vanish, dissolve in the crucible of racial and ethnic codification. Ever since becoming aware of socialization based upon skin color, I have been a fiend for the appropriate forum. Yet, never have I found it.

Paris was a unique city. Yet, an undercurrent of racism ran through it. Being privy to this prejudicial treatment given Africans, West Indians, and Maghrebians, I had to be cautious of how I maneuvered through Paris lest I be mistaken as one of them. The new humanity that I experienced required me to constantly invoke my American identity. Strangely enough, I embodied more of what Alain Locke called a "New Negro" in Paris, to the extent that I prioritized my Americanism. To wear American citizenship as a gold star of honor in my mind was not saying much.

For me, this reinforced how much of a matrix Black people existed in the world over. As long as I did so, a space existed for me to celebrate my so-called blackness and to pursue my attempts at cultural production. My heartfelt centuries of oppressions seen and unseen. How could I look at Paris as a symbol of freedom and liberation, if I had to maneuver in such a way as not to be mistaken as a person of African ancestry? An American? Who am I truly? This epiphany settled on my chest, causing me to see Sankofa with a renewed vision.

I discovered the French hierarchy places the Arab at the bottom, followed by the Africans, and then Afro-Caribbeans. The French, however, are willing to make concessions for African-Americans because of their disconnection from their history of colonization. France has held a deep admiration for Black American culture. But the problem with this adulation of Black American culture is that, they are only accepting of a segment of the Black experience and pigeon hole it into a musical art form; whether that be Jazz or Hip=Hop; conscious or not. We are magnanimously respected and revered for our entertainment contribution and status. Entertainment in the French mind does not challenge the socio-economic or political status quo.

Nevertheless, I was not living at the turn of the nineteenth century or during the decadent '50s, so Parisians were quick to peg me as an athlete or a rap artist. At times, I felt like James Baldwin, when Parisians had asked him, "*Jouez-vous la trompette* (Do you play the trumpet)?" And like Baldwin, I felt like telling them: "*Non, nous ne jouons pas la trompette* (No, we do not play the trumpet)." Of course, Parisians misidentifying me as a performer (of whatever sort) irritated me to no end. In such instances, I sometimes recited the military triumphs of James Reese Europe and the 369th Infantry Regiment (known as the Harlem Hellfighters) during WW I. After the Armistice, the Hellfighters were awarded the Croix de Guerre, having spent 191 days in action, the longest single stretch of combat of any group of American soldiers, black or white, in the Great War. Or, I would inform my inquisitors of the 88 pilots in the all-black 332nd Fighter Group who, along with Colonel Benjamin O. Davis, Jr., received the Distinguished Flying Cross for more than three thousand missions in Europe and for shooting down almost three hundred enemy planes in WW II.

At the turn of the millennium, I am in Paris, observing the Fête de la Musique of 1998 and the celebration of the 150th anniversary of the emancipation from slavery called *L'Honneur et le Respect* (Honor and Respect). Along with family and friends, I march through the streets with African people from all over the world. A myriad's myriad don the tattered clothes of Maroons, with their hands shackled in chains, carrying torches that represent the African's final passage from slave castle doors of no return to the plantations of the New World.

In 1898, W.E.B. Du Bois described the Champs Élysées to a Black audience in Louisville, Kentucky as "the center of the aesthetic culture of the 19th century." And today, one hundred years later, I am surrounded by a multitude of native African tongues, but silence stills them, divided by the ghost of linguistic enslavement. All I hear is French. Ironically, we march for freedom from chattel slavery, but mental slavery has shackled these tongues. It is a strange dilemma to walk in two worlds, speak and function in two worlds, fight for acceptance and freedom in two worlds, and still ultimately feel like you do not belong to either of the worlds you fight to belong. Is freedom what we really fight for? Or, are we longing to be recognized as humans in a world that perpetuates the badge of invisibility?

I wonder if the French and other Europeans can honor and respect Blacks with colonial tongues.

EuroStar: Gare du Nord

A phone call is patched from England
My family awaits my arrival

A three hour travel through the Chunnel via
Londres
First class accommodations, great service and
respect

Gare du Nord (Les Lignes Grandes), one of the 6
majors
Paris, the City of Light

I touched ground, feeling a sense of relief and
accomplishment
Home I was, a dream fulfilled, no longer a
conversation, reality

I could feel instantly, the spirits of my ancestors
Langston, Himes, Baldwin, McKay, Tanner, Bearden,
Jones, & Baker

Relieved to know, my heart felt
Beginning of a journey, fulfilled

Words could not describe this sensation, this feeling
This euphoria this desire

The potential to become another
Black-American expatriate

To be alive in Paris!   Paris?

To experience the vibrancy my ancestors
Eloquently wrote about and depicted in prose

Novels, arts, letters, music, paintings, sculptures,
poems
I didn't feel any racial conundrums

I thought of the Louvre: Mona Lisa, Egyptian
artifacts
Bastille, Pigalle, Montmatre, the Champs Elysees,
L'Arc De Triomphe

Place de Clichy: Alexander Dumas and his Three
Musketeers
The Count of Monte Cristo: the Chateau D'IF

The Monaco: wine, world, word, women, weed –
(journaling)
Notre Dame, the Seine River, Versailles, the Latin
Quarter

I felt like I had arrived in a French speaking New
York, overwhelmed

City of Light was much more tantalizing
Open fluid, liberating

All is this opened to me, once I left Gare du Nord
I was in heaven and she blessed me with Paris

Nathan Jones is a poet, a storyteller, and the author of Revolutionary Erotica, Black Man in Europe: Micro-Volume I, and Excerpts From My Soul: Read Without Prejudice. He is an educator who takes pleasure in working with urban youth in his community. He currently resides in Oakland, California.

Other Books by Nathan Jones:
Revolutionary Erotica and Other Poems
Black Man In Europe: Micro-Volume I
Excerpts From My Soul: Read Without Prejudice

Forthcoming Projects from Nathan Jones:
Letters To My Daughter: How A Dad Became A
Father
In The Moment: A Collection Of Poetry
The Paris Chronicles
Love's Reflection
Letters: Voices From The Past

Connect with Nathan Jones Online
www.sajetanira.com